More Home Cooking IN A HURRY

Sarah Howell

BROADMAN PRESS
Nashville, Tennessee

4270-03
ISBN: 0-8054-7003-4

Dewey Decimal Classification: 641.5
Subject Heading: COOKERY
Library of Congress Catalog Card Number: 86-9716
Printed in the United States of America

All Scripture quotations are taken from
the King James Version of the Bible.

Library of Congress Cataloging-in-Publication Data

Howell, Sarah, 1929-
More home cooking in a hurry.

Includes index.
1. Cookery. I. Title.
TX715.H8619 1986 641.5′55 86-9716
ISBN 0-8054-7003-4

To my niece, Melanie Smith.

Introduction

Walt Whitman said, "The art of art . . . is simplicity." Truly, the artist must simplify to get down to the root meaning of what he is doing.

As with any art, the art of cooking can be simplified. There is no need for hassle and frustration in order to get fabulous food on the table.

Simply delicious food can be fixed fast when meals are planned, recipes simplified, and equipment used to save time.

The goal is to have nutritious, delicious food on the table in minutes. With that in mind, I have planned menus which look good, taste good, and are good for you, with foods that can be fixed fast. The recipes are neither complicated nor time consuming.

This book is for nutrition-minded people who are in a hurry.

There are menus and recipes for breakfast, lunch, and dinner. Most meals can be prepared in fifteen to forty-five minutes.

The breakfast and lunch menus are for people who "eat on the run," as well as for those who linger over a meal.

It has been a challenge to plan foods which are nutritionally adequate, taste good, and can be eaten on the run. Food is to be enjoyed even by busy people.

Meals in Minutes

These menus and recipes are for busy people who want quick-to-prepare, delicious meals in minutes. These food suggestions can be fixed fast in nutritionally balanced meals.

Plan to eat with pleasure—in minutes—be it breakfast, lunch, or dinner.

Brown Bagging

People who take their lunch to work or school need suffer through no more boring brown-bag lunches, nor choke on another dry sandwich. This chapter has a multitude of ideas, menus, and recipes for preparing luscious sack lunches.

Many of the same menus could be used for picnics, packing in the car for a trip, or backpacking.

Fast Breakfast

Food for breakfast doesn't have to take a long time to prepare. Neither does it have to be the traditional breakfast. If your schedule limits the time you have to prepare breakfast, you'll love these ideas.

Time-Saving Appliances

Freeze with Ease
Points on Processors
Memo on the Microwave

Three time-saving appliances are discussed. None are necessary for preparing food in this book, although their use is suggested in some recipes as time savers.

Special plan-ahead recipes for the freezer are given.

Cheese Is a Breeze

This chapter is included because cheese is a fabulous fast food which can be used as an appetizer, main course, snack, or dessert.

The cheese chart is a handy guide; it lists the names, pronunciations, tastes, and uses of most cheeses you would encounter at a store.

Contents

1
Meals in Minutes

These menus and recipes are for busy people who want simple-to-prepare, simply delicious food to eat—in a hurry.

People are busy with careers, home, and community activities. There is pressure to balance responsibilities to others and ourselves—to live full, meaningful lives. Everyone has a physical need to eat well, keep weight under control, and exercise, and an emotional need to enjoy the food he eats.

Good, well-balanced meals must be planned, and meal planning takes time. These menus eliminate that time-consuming chore.

Most of the meals can be prepared in fifteen to forty-five minutes.

Recipes are listed with each menu. This arrangement saves time, but does not prevent one from mixing and matching recipes in the book.

If you want a menu or recipe using a certain food, such as chicken, look in the Index under Chicken.

The index lists all food in alphabetical order—for instance, Apple(s), Apricot(s), Artichoke(s), Asparagus, Avocado, Banana, Bean(s), Bean Sprouts, etc.

Foods are also listed by categories—for instance, Barbecue, Biscuits, Bread(s), Cake(s), Casserole(s), Cheese(s), Fruit(s), Meat(s), Vegetable(s), etc.

To save time, keep a supply of basic food ingredients in the kitchen. This will eliminate trips to the grocery, and every trip saved is time saved.

A modest supply would include canned fruits, meats, soups, and vegetables; basic dry ingredients such as flour, sugar, rice, cereal, crackers, cookies, herbs, and spices. If you have space, keep frozen food on hand. A freezer is truly a time-saving appliance. Not only do you store bought food in it; but you may also use it for planned-over food. A recipe can be doubled and half frozen for future use. There is one preparation time for two meals.

It is amazing how many fabulous, fast-cooked meals one can prepare on the spur of the moment from a basic food supply.

"Live with a thrifty, not a needy Fate;
Small shots paid often, waste a vast estate."

Robert Herrick, 1648

"Every house where love abides and friendship is a guest, is surely home, . . . and there the heart can rest."

Henry Van Dyke

"If this world affords true happiness, it is to be found in a house where love and confidence increase with the years, where the necessities of life come without severe strain, where luxuries enter only after their cost has been carefully considered."

Edward Newton

Broiled Steak
Broiler Creamed Corn
Zucchini-Okra-Tomato Salad
(see Index)
Blackberry Doughnut

This meal can be prepared in 30 minutes. Purchase bread if desired.

Broiled Steak

Beef steak for 4 (sirloin, T-bone, Porter-house, or tenderloin)
2 cloves garlic
1½ to 2 tablespoons Worcester-shire sauce
Butter or margarine
Salt
Pepper

Place garlic in bottom of broiler pan; crush cloves using side of knife. Place Worcestershire sauce in bottom of pan with garlic.

Dip steak (top and bottom) into sauce and garlic mixture. Remove steak and place on broiler rack.

(If you are preparing the Broiler Creamed Corn, place it into bottom of broiler pan at this time.)

Dot top of steak with butter; add pepper. Broil 4-5 minutes; turn. Dot that side with butter; add dashes of salt and pepper. Broil until desired doneness.

Broiler Creamed Corn

1 can (17 oz.) cream-style corn
Paprika

This corn picks up the flavors from the steak, garlic, Worcestershire sauce, salt, pepper, and butter. It needs no seasonings other than a little paprika.

Open can of corn; place contents in bottom of broiler pan (with leftover garlic and Worcestershire sauce); stir. Add a few dashes of paprika.

Place broiler rack over the corn. Broil steak following the recipe above. Serves 4.

Blackberry Doughnut

4 doughnuts
3 to 4 tablespoons blackberry jam per serving

Split doughnuts in half horizontally. Spread each cut side with jam.

Place on broiler rack. Broil one minute. Serve warm.

Hint: Heat these the last minute while the steak cooks.

When broiling meat on grill, rub grate first with fat. Meat will not stick to a greased grill.

Pan-Broiled Shrimp
Mushroom-Spinach Salad
Crusty Italian Bread
(Purchase)
Cheesecake
(see Index)
or
Grapes with Brick Cheese

Set cheese out of the refrigerator when starting to prepare food. Brick improves in flavor if served at room temperature.

Pan-Broiled Shrimp

Shrimp (5 or 6 per person)
1 stick margarine or butter
1 or 2 cloves garlic, minced
4 tablespoons lemon juice
1/4 teaspoon dill weed
1 teaspoon salt
1/8 teaspoon pepper

Use uncooked shrimp—fresh or frozen. Remove the shell, but leave the tail and last section on. Incise the back, removing the black vein.

Melt butter in pan; add seasonings. Stir-fry shrimp until they are cooked (3-5 minutes).

Mushroom-Spinach Salad

Spinach
½ onion, sliced into rings
⅓ cup sliced fresh mushrooms
1 teaspoon Worcestershire sauce
¼ teaspoon thyme
4 tablespoons salad oil
2 tablespoons lemon juice
1 teaspoon soy sauce
Dash of salt

Combine mushrooms and onion with seasonings.

Break spinach into bite-size pieces. Pour other ingredients on top.

Baked Country Ham Slice

Sweet Potato Casserole | **Baked Apples**
(see Index)

Celery Sticks | **Olives**

Biscuits | **Jelly**

(Purchase or see Index)

Baked Country Ham Slice

1 slice country ham approximately 3/8 inch thick

Trim off outer skin of ham, but do not remove the fat. Score edge to prevent buckling.

Wipe ham slice with a damp paper towel, then place into a greased shallow baking pan. Cover container with aluminum foil; bake in a 325° oven for 25 minutes. Serve warm with red gravy from the bottom of the pan.

Sweet Potato Casserole

1 1/2 cups cooked sweet potatoes
1/2 cup orange juice or pineapple juice
1/3 cup brown sugar
1/4 teaspoon salt
1/2 teaspoon cinnamon
1/2 teaspoon nutmeg or mace
Miniature marshmallows

Place all ingredients except marshmallows into the bowl of a food processor or mixer. Whip to combine.

Pour into a greased casserole dish. Top with a few marshmallows.

Bake 25 minutes in a 350° oven.

"There is always a best way to do everything, if it be to boil an egg."

Emerson

"Cultivate simplicity."

Coleridge

"Let all things be done decently and in order."
1 Corinthians 14:18

"Better is a dinner of herbs where love is, than a stalled ox and hatred therewith."

Proverbs 15:17

Turkey Breast Steaks with Fruit
Quick-Cook Rice
Lettuce and Cheese Salad
(see Index)
Vanilla Ice Cream with Pirouette Cookies
(Purchase)

This is a delectable meal which can be prepared in 30 minutes or less.

Put the rice on to cook first. It takes 10 minutes to prepare.

Next, prepare the salad.

The turkey breasts cook so fast that they should be prepared last and served warm.

Quick-Cook Rice

Follow package directions for preparation.

Turkey Breast Steaks with Fruit

Look in the poultry section of the meat department for turkey breast steaks. Sometimes they are called turkey tenderloin.

They are thin (approximately ¼ inch) slices of fresh turkey breast.

6-8 turkey steak slices
3 tablespoons butter
1 tablespoon oil
2 cloves garlic, minced
¼ teaspoon celery seed
½ tablespoon cornstarch
1 tablespoon brown sugar
1 teaspoon soy sauce
½ teaspoon ground ginger
1 can (15½ oz.) pineapple chunks
¾ cup seedless, green grapes

Drain the liquid from the pineapple into a small bowl; set pineapple aside. Add the cornstarch, sugar, soy sauce, and ginger to the liquid; stir to blend; set aside.

Rinse turkey slices; pat dry. Sprinkle with celery seed.

Place butter, oil, and garlic into a large frying pan; add turkey slices. Cook on medium heat 3 minutes. Turn. Cook 2 to 3 more minutes. Remove to a platter.

Add the cornstarch mixture to the frying pan. Turn heat to low. Cook, stirring constantly until glassy looking (approximately 1 minute). Add the grapes and pineapple chunks. Stir to blend and heat. Pour over the turkey steaks. Serves 4.

"Except the Lord build the house,
they labor in vain that build it."

Psalm 123:1

"He that is of a merry heart hath a continual feast."

Proverbs 15:15

Broiled Flounder
Broiled Tomatoes
Slaw
Quick Banana Pudding
or
Orange Sherbet

To prepare this meal quickly: Marinade the fish first; then prepare the pudding and slaw. The flounder and tomatoes cook in such a short time that it is best to have all the other food prepared before putting them under the broiler.

Broiled Flounder

Flounder fillet for 2 people (Other fish might be substituted.)

Paprika

Marinade

1/2 cup milk
1/2 teaspoon dried onion flakes
1/2 teaspoon salt
1 tablespoon lemon juice
1/4 teaspoon dried tarragon
Freshly ground pepper

Combine ingredients for the marinade in a glass dish.

Rinse the flounder; place in the marinade until you are ready to broil it.

To Broil:

Brush the broiler rack with oil to prevent sticking. Place the fish on the rack; brush flounder with oil or butter. Broil 2 minutes on each side.

Sprinkle with paprika before serving.

Hint: Avoid overcooking. The fish is done when the translucent fish turns opaque. It is better to have slightly undercooked fish than to overcook it. This is a delicate, tender meat.

Broiled Tomatoes

1 small or 1/2 large tomato per serving
Butter
Salt and pepper

Leave skins on the tomatoes. Cut large ones in half; broil cut side up. Small ones are cooked whole. Cut blossom end off, and score tops of small tomatoes.

Dip each tomato into the fish marinade. Place on the broiler rack; sprinkle with salt and pepper; then dot each tomato with butter.

Broil approximately 5 minutes.

Slaw

Cabbage
1 stalk celery
1 carrot
Alfalfa bean sprouts

Dressing

2 or 3 tablespoons mayonnaise
1 tablespoon vinegar
1/8 teaspoon dill weed
1/8 teaspoon salt
Freshly ground pepper

Combine ingredients for the dressing in a bowl.

Peel carrot; grate. Grate or slice the cabbage and celery. Combine these vegetables with the dressing; toss to coat well with the dressing.

Add the bean sprouts last. Toss gently. They do not need to be totally covered with the dressing.

If desired, sprinkle paprika on top of the salad before serving. Serves 2.

Quick Banana Pudding

1 package (3 1/8 oz.) vanilla pudding and pie filling
2 bananas
Vanilla wafers

Prepare pie filling, following package directions. Remove from heat.

Use four individual glass bowls or one large one.

Arrange a layer of wafers in the bottom of the bowl. Cover the wafers with banana slices; then cover with the custard.

Add another layer of vanilla wafers, bananas, and pudding mix. The pudding should be on top. Let stand until the wafers are slightly softened.

Some people like whipped topping or cream on top, although it is not necessary. Serves 4.

Fabulous Breast of Chicken
Carrot-Apple-Orange Salad
Parmesan French Bread
Ice Cream Pie

(see Index)

(or purchase pie)

Fabulous Chicken

- Boned chicken for 2, cut into small pieces
- 3 stalks celery, chopped
- 1 tablespoon oil
- 1 tablespoon butter or margarine
- 1 tablespoon chopped parsley
- 1/2 teaspoon thyme
- 1/4 cup flour
- 1/2 teaspoon salt
- 1/4 teaspoon pepper
- 1/4 cup toasted almonds

Wash and drain chicken. Cut away any cartilage.

Combine in a small bag the flour, salt, pepper, thyme, and parsley. Toss chicken to coat. Shake each piece to remove excess flour.

Heat fat over medium-high heat. Add the chicken and celery. Stir and cook until golden brown—5 to 7 minutes. Add almonds; toss in pan. Serves 2.

Carrot-Apple-Orange Salad

2 carrots (or 1½ if large)
1 apple
1 can (11 oz.) Mandarin orange segments
1 teaspoon lemon juice
¼ cup mayonnaise
Dash of salt

Dice apple, removing core and seeds; leave peeling on. Combine ingredients. Toss to coat with salad dressing. Serve on lettuce, bean sprouts, or in a bowl. Serves 2.

Parmesan French Bread

1 can (11oz.) refrigerated French bread loaf
Parmesan cheese

Preheat oven to 350°F. Butter a cookie sheet.

Open can; place bread on baking pan. With kitchen shears, snip 6 diagonal cuts in the loaf. Sprinkle grated Parmesan cheese into the cuts.

Bake approximately 30 minutes in a 350°F. oven.

Hint: For garlic bread, brush on a small amount of garlic juice.

Ham with Honey

Southern Green Beans **Sliced Tomatoes**

Lettuce and Cheese Salad

Rolls or Biscuits

(Purchase)

Very Berry Compote

A quick-cook meal that you will enjoy serving to family or friends.

Look for fully cooked, boneless ham in the ham section of the meat department. The hams come in sizes which will serve as few as 4 to 6 people or enough for a banquet.

They are fully cooked and lend themselves to a multitude of varied menus.

The cloves, mustard, and honey added to the ham in this recipe enhance its flavor tremendously.

Ham with Honey

- 2 slices cooked ham (about 1/2 inch thick)
- 2 tablespoons honey
- 1 tablespoon prepared mustard
- 1/4 teaspoon ground cloves

Combine honey, mustard, and cloves. Spread over top of ham slices, coating them. Heat ham in a microwave oven until warm (1-2 minutes).

or

Heat ham in a 350°F. oven until warm (approximately 8 minutes). Serves 4.

Southern Green Beans

1 can (16 oz.) green beans
1 tablespoon bacon drippings
1 whole hot pepper or a dash of hot pepper sauce
½ teaspoon salt

Heat green beans and seasonings together, using the range or microwave oven. The microwave takes 3 to 4 minutes, and the beans should be stirred halfway through the cooking.

When cooking on top of a range, cover and simmer 6-10 minutes. Serves 3-4.

Lettuce and Cheese Salad

Lettuce of your choice (for example, romaine, iceberg, endive)
French dressing
¼ cup Cheddar cheese, grated
⅓ cup Camembert cheese, cut into small pieces

Tear lettuce into bite-size pieces; place on salad plates. Combine cheeses and arrange on top of lettuce. Pour a small amount of French dressing over the top of each salad. Serves 4.

Very Berry Compote

1 cup strawberries
1 cup blueberries
3 pear halves (canned)
1 to 2 teaspoons sugar if desired (not necessary)

Wash and drain berries. Cut strawberries in half or leave whole.

Cut pears into bite-size pieces. Combine fruits and sugar; toss gently. Pour pear juice over the fruits.

Serve chilled in glass compotes.

"Peace be to this house."

Luke 10:5

"Some have meat but cannot eat;
Some could eat but have no meat;
We have meat and all can eat;
Blest, therefore, be God for our meat."

Unknown, *The Selkirk Grace*, 1650

"Some people have food, but no appetite; others have appetite, but no food; I have both. The Lord be praised!"

Oliver Cromwell

Sautéed Chicken Livers
Corn on the Cob
Orange-Avocado Salad
or
Head Lettuce Salad
Cheesecake
(see Index)
or
Macaroons
(Purchase)

Liver is a highly nutritious food which is seldom eaten by most people.

If you dislike the taste of liver, try this recipe. It will turn you into a "liver lover" because it is flavorful and not greasy like most fried liver.

Sautéed Chicken Livers

- 8 chicken livers
- 1/4 cup flour
- 1/4 teaspoon salt
- 1 tablespoon chopped fresh parsley
- Dash of pepper
- 2 tablespoons cooking oil
- 1/2 teaspoon Worcestershire sauce

Rinse livers and drain. Combine flour, salt, pepper, and parsley in a small bag. Add the chicken livers; toss to coat.

Heat cooking oil to medium-high. Add the chicken livers. Stir and turn until lightly browned all over. *Do not cook until hard.* Chicken livers should be soft and tender.

Turn the heat to simmer; add 1/4 cup water and Worcestershire sauce. Cover and steam 2-3 minutes. Serves 2.

Hint: Puncture each liver with a fork to check popping.

Corn on Cob

The best corn is freshly picked and shucked. Corn starts to lose some of its sweet flavor within a few minutes of harvest.

If the fresh corn in a market looks dry, you will get better flavor from frozen.

When using frozen corn, follow the package directions.

This recipe is for cooking fresh corn. It is sweet and tender. Serve it warm, and pass the butter.

2 ears corn with shucks on
1 teaspoon salt

Shuck the corn and remove the silks. Rinse, and remove any blemish.

Bring water to boil. Add salt and corn. Cover the pan, and cook on low 6 to 8 minutes—until tender. Serves 2.

Orange-Avocado Salad

This is a colorful, delicious, quickly prepared salad.

1 large or 2 small oranges
1/2 avocado
Lettuce
French dressing

Place lettuce on individual salad plates.

Peel orange; slice into circles; remove seeds. Place on lettuce.

Cut avocado in half. Peel that half and slice into strips. Place slices on top of orange circles.

Drizzle a small amount of French dressing over the top.

Hint: Tightly cover and refrigerate the other avocado half for future use.

Tuna-Tossed Salad
Crescent Cheese Rolls
(or purchase rolls)
Sherbet

This is a super-speedy meal which can be prepared in 15 minutes or less.

Not only is it easy and fast to prepare; there is only one bowl to wash for the meat and vegetables.

Tuna-Tossed Salad

1 can (6½ oz.) chunk light tuna, chilled
Vegetables for tossed salad
½ teaspoon basil or dill weed
Italian salad dressing
Dash salt
Dash pepper

Prepare vegetables of your choice for a tossed salad (lettuce, tomatoes, celery, squash, etc.).

Cut or break vegetables into bite-size pieces. Place in a salad bowl.

Drain oil from tuna. Add tuna to salad. Pour on a small amount of salad dressing; add seasonings. Toss gently. Serves 2.

Crescent Cheese Rolls

1 can (8 oz.) crescent dinner rolls
½ cup sharp Cheddar cheese, grated
Dash paprika
Celery seeds

Preheat oven to 350°F.

Open can of rolls. Separate dough into four sections. Stretch dough. Sprinkle with cheese, celery seed, and paprika.

Starting on the wide side, roll each section jellyroll fashion. Cut the 4 rolls into 16 individual rolls.

Bake 10 minutes on aluminum foil-lined cookie sheet. Serve warm.

Set priorities. Decide what *must* be done; what I *want* done; and what I can leave *undone*.

"Home is the resort of love, of joy, of peace, and plenty where supporting and supported, polished friends and dearest relative mingle into bliss."

Thomson

"The wealth of a soul is measured by how much it can feel; its poverty by how little."

W. R. Alger

Oriental Dinner
Rice
Apricots and Fortune Cookies

Cooking time for this meal should be 15 minutes if instant rice is used.

Oriental Dinner

½ pound sirloin steak (or other tender cut)
Cooking oil
1 medium tomato cut into thin wedges
1 (10 oz.) package Chinese-style stir-fry vegetables
1 teaspoon soy sauce

Cut steak into very thin slices. It is easier to cut if first partially frozen, then sliced diagonally across the grain.

Open Chinese-style vegetables. Remove seasoning packet from box. Sprinkle seasonings and soy sauce on steak slices.

Stir-fry meat in 1 or 2 tablespoons cooking oil. Remove meat from pan.

Place Chinese vegetables into pan. Cook, following directions on package. When vegetables are nearly tender, return meat to the pan and add tomato; toss to heat. Serve over rice. Two servings.

Shrimp-Tomato Salad
Cheddar Biscuits
or
Assorted Crackers
Pound Cake with Butternut Sauce

Shrimp-Tomato Salad

4 tomatoes
1 (4½ oz.) can shrimp
1 (5 oz.) can water chestnuts
1 or 2 green onions
½ cup mayonnaise
1 tablespoon fresh dill weed (or ½ tablespoon dried)
1 tablespoon capers, drained

Rinse and drain shrimp. Chop water chestnuts and onions. Combine all ingredients; toss gently.

Slice stem end from tomatoes. Cut each tomato into segments, forming a flower shape. Do not cut all the way through the base.

Fill center of each tomato with shrimp mixture. Serves 4.

Cheddar Biscuits

1 can (9½ oz.) refrigerated biscuits
½ cup grated Cheddar cheese
Milk

Preheat oven to 450°F.

Line shallow baking pan with aluminum foil. Separate each biscuit in half; place on foil-covered pan.

Brush top of each biscuit with milk. Sprinkle tops with cheese.

Bake until golden brown. Serve warm.

Butternut Sauce

½ cup chocolate sauce

¼ cup crunchy peanut butter

Combine sauce and peanut butter. Heat to melt peanut butter. (A microwave oven is great for this.)

Pour over pound cake while sauce is warm.

Hint: This sauce is also good over ice cream, angelfood cake, and fruit (try it with baked pears).

"This world is so full of care and sorrow that it is a gracious debt we owe to one another to discover the bright crystals of delight hidden in somber circumstances and irksome tasks."

Helen Keller

"He is happiest, king or peasant, who finds his happiness at home."

Goethe

Sliced Baked Ham
Zucchini-Okra-Tomato Salad
Corn Chips
Rye Bread
Ice Cream

This is another super-speedy meal which is good and good for you. The salad has three vegetables; and the menu also includes sources of milk, meat, and bread.

Zucchini-Okra-Tomato Salad

1 zucchini squash
4 or 5 pickled okra pods
1 large or 2 small tomatoes
3 or 4 tablespoons sour cream
1/4 teaspoon salt
1/2 teaspoon basil
Freshly ground black pepper

Wash squash, do not peel; cut into bite-size chunks.

Cut pickled okra into bite-size pieces.

Wash tomato, remove stem end, do not peel; cut into bite-size chunks.

Toss all ingredients together. Serve on lettuce leaf or bed of parsley. Serves 2 or 3.

Grilled Turkey Breast
Grilled Eggplant
Cranberry Sauce Olives
Asian Salad
Hard French Rolls
Black Cherry Yogurt Ice Cream
(Purchase)

This turkey and eggplant are simply delicious cooked over charcoal. Total cooking time for each is 6 or 8 minutes—3 or 4 minutes on each side.

Grilled Turkey Breast

Buy thinly sliced fresh turkey breast. Make the marinade first and let the turkey soak 15-30 minutes before cooking. In fact, it could be soaked several hours, then cooked at serving time if that fits your schedule better.

Marinade

1/2 cup salad oil
1/4 cup vinegar or lemon juice
1 clove garlic, crushed
1/2 teaspoon salt
Freshly ground pepper
1/2 tablespoon crushed, dried thyme
1/2 tablespoon dried celery leaves

Combine ingredients for the marinade in a glass bowl. Place turkey slices in the marinade. They should be covered with the mixture. This should be enough marinade for two or three servings. Let meat absorb flavors.

Cook over glowing coals 4-5 minutes on each side. Brush meat with marinade as it cooks.

Hint: A wire barbecue basket is a useful (not necessary) piece of equipment for cooking small steaks.

Grilled Eggplant

1/2 fresh eggplant
1/4 cup flour
1/2 teaspoon salt
1/4 teaspoon pepper
Cooking oil
Parmesan cheese

Peel eggplant; cut into half-inch slices. Soak a few minutes in a bowl of cool salted water to remove any bitterness. Let eggplant soak while combining the flour, salt, and pepper.

Drain eggplant slices and pat dry on paper towel. Dredge slices in the flour mixture.

Brush slices with cooking oil. Broil over charcoal, turning once.

Sprinkle with Parmesan cheese when the slices are turned. Serve warm. Serves 2.

Asian Salad

5 oz. pineapple chunks
5 oz. Mandarin orange slices
1/2 avocado
1 tablespoon mayonnaise

Thin the mayonnaise with one tablespoon juice from the canned Mandarin oranges.

Cut the avocado into bite-size pieces. Combine all ingredients; toss gently.

Hint: Miniature marshmallows may be added to this salad if desired.

Pan-Broiled Filet Mignon
Herb Steamed Tomatoes
Asparagus Vinaigrette
or
Green Salad
Pineapple and Edam Cheese

Prepare the asparagus salad first, so it can chill in the refrigerator while preparing other food.

Pan-Broiled Filet Mignon

2 filet mignon
2 tablespoons butter
1 tablespoon oil
2 chopped shallots
Salt
Pepper
1 tablespoon vinegar
1 cup sliced fresh mushrooms (optional)

Warm oil and butter over medium-high heat. Sprinkle salt and pepper on both sides of each steak.

Place steaks into hot pan. Cook 2 to 4 minutes on each side (until lightly browned). Remove meat from pan.

Add shallots and mushrooms; stir-fry until golden—but not brown. Place vegetables on top of steaks.

Put vinegar into the pan; stir and scrape bottom; then pour over meat. Serves 2.

Herb Steamed Tomatoes

2 medium-size tomatoes
1/3 cup water
1/4 cup fresh parsley
Dash pepper
2 tablespoons chopped onion
2 tablespoons fresh basil
1 tablespoon butter
Dash salt

Wash tomatoes. Cut off stem end (top). Make 2 half-inch cuts on each tomato.

Chop parsley, onion, and basil; place into a saucepan with the water. Place tomatoes on bed of herbs. Sprinkle each tomato with salt and pepper and top with butter.

Cover pan; simmer 3-5 minutes. Serve tomatoes whole with herbs on top.

Asparagus Vinaigrette

Fresh asparagus
1/2 cup salad oil
1/4 cup vinegar
1/4 cup chopped parsley
1 crushed clove garlic
1/4 teaspoon salt
Freshly ground pepper

Wash asparagus; break off woody portions. Place in a covered container with 2 or 3 tablespoons water. Microwave 6 minutes, stirring once.

Pour off water. Combine other ingredients; pour them over warm asparagus. Chill.

Hint: Canned asparagus may be substituted for fresh.

Chicken Livers with Mushroom Sauce
Rice
Banana-Celery Salad
or
Sliced Tomatoes
Strawberry Yogurt Ice Cream
(Purchase)

Chicken Livers with Mushroom Sauce

Chicken livers are high in iron, protein, and vitamins. Eat these with pleasure!

8 chicken livers
1 cup chicken broth or bouillon

Bring broth to boil. Add the chicken livers. Turn the heat to simmer. Cook 12-15 minutes until tender.

While the livers are cooking prepare the mushroom sauce.

Mushroom Sauce

1 can (10½ oz.) mushroom soup
½ can milk or broth from livers
1 teaspoon dried onion flakes
Dash of salt and pepper
½ teaspoon dried celery leaves or parsley
¼ teaspoon Worcestershire sauce

Combine ingredients; stir to blend. Simmer 5 minutes. Add the chicken livers and serve over rice.

or

Place the cooked livers on a bed of rice and pour the sauce on top. Serves 2.

Banana-Celery Salad

1 banana
Mayonnaise
1 or 2 stalks of celery
Dates if desired

Cut the celery into bite-size pieces. Peel and cut the banana into circles. Add the dates.

Toss gently with just enough mayonnaise to moisten.

Serve in lettuce cups or from a bowl. Serves 2.

Oriental Omelet

Cherry Tomatoes Bell Pepper Rings

Chilled Mandarin Orange Segments

Ginger Cookies

This omelet is a meal in one dish, although you might wish to add a bread or rice to this menu.

Oriental Omelet

4 slices bacon
2 stalks celery, chopped
3/4 cup sliced fresh mushrooms
1/4 cup chopped onion
4 eggs
1 tablespoon soy sauce
1 cup fresh mung bean sprouts

Cook bacon in frying pan; remove and drain. Leave bacon fat in the pan. Place the celery, mushrooms, and onion in the skillet. Stir-fry until crisp-tender (4-5 minutes).

Beat eggs with soy sauce; pour over vegetables in the pan. Cook on low until eggs are firm on one side. Add the bean sprouts; fold eggs over omelet style. Serves 2 or 3.

Sliced Smoked Turkey
Carrot-Okra-Tomato Salad
Potato Chips
Pound Cake with Butternut Sauce

(see Index)

Pick up some smoked turkey at the deli. Add the bread of your choice.

You will enjoy this meal in minutes.

Carrot-Okra-Tomato Salad

2 carrots
4 or 5 pickled okra pods
1 large tomato
1/4 teaspoon salt
1/2 teaspoon basil
1/4 teaspoon pepper
3 or 4 tablespoons sour cream

Wash carrots; peel, and cut into bite-size pieces.

Cut pickled okra into bite-size pieces.

Wash tomato; remove stem end, cut into bite-size chunks.

Place all ingredients into a bowl; toss to combine. Serves 2.

Cheese Breeze
Baked Celery
or
Marinated Green Peas
Carrot Sticks Pickles
Minted Baked Pears

This oven meal can be prepared hours ahead, refrigerated, then cooked when needed. If necessary, it can be prepared the day before. That makes it a real time-management winner.

Cheese Breeze

8 slices white bread
1/3 pound sliced Cheddar cheese
3 eggs
2 dashes red hot sauce or 1 teaspoon prepared mustard
1 2/3 cups milk
1/2 teaspoon salt
1 or 2 tablespoons chopped onion

Grease a casserole dish. Place half of the bread on bottom of container; cover with sliced cheese. Add another layer of bread and cheese.

Beat eggs; combine with other ingredients; then pour over the cheese and bread. Allow time for the bread to soak up some of the liquid.

Bake 45-50 minutes in a 350°F. oven. Serves 4.

Baked Celery

7 or 8 stalks of celery, sliced
1 can (10½ oz.) mushroom soup
½ can milk
1 can (8 oz.) sliced water chestnuts
1 (2 oz.) jar diced pimientos
1 tablespoon chopped chives
½ teaspoon salt
1 tablespoon butter

Combine ingredients. Pour into a 1-quart buttered casserole. Sprinkle top with bread crumbs and paprika. Bake 35-45 minutes in a 350°F. oven.

Marinated Green Peas

1 can (16 oz.) green peas
1 clove garlic, minced
¼ teaspoon celery seed
¼ cup lemon juice
⅓ cup salad oil
Dash pepper
¼ teaspoon salt

Drain peas. Place liquid in a pan; add other ingredients except peas. Bring fluid to a boil; add peas. Remove from heat; chill. Serve cold. 4 servings.

Carrot Sticks

Wash carrots; peel. Slice into long, thin slices. Cover with ice water. Store in refrigerator until time to serve. Drain water when ready to serve.

Minted Baked Pears

These pears may be cooked in the oven with the other food, or in a microwave oven on high for 4-5 minutes.

4 fresh pears
1/2 cup water
1 tablespoon honey
1 tablespoon lemon juice
1/2 teaspoon mace
1/2 teaspoon cinnamon
1/3 cup mint jelly
2 drops green food coloring

Combine all ingredients except pears. Microwave 1 1/2 minutes on high.

Peel pears; slice in half removing stem and seeds.

Place center cut side down in a dish. Pour other ingredients over the pears; cover. Microwave 2 minutes on high. Baste with liquid; turn; cover; cook 2 more minutes.

Fresh carrots are nearly always cheaper than canned or frozen, and can be purchased year-round.

"Love is caring and sharing."

Howell

"Set thine house in order."

2 Kings 20:1

Chicken Salad
Apricot Bran Muffins
(see Index)
(or purchase bread)
Frozen Peanut Butter Dessert
(see Index)
or
Purchased Pound Cake with Ice Cream

Chicken Salad

2 cups diced cooked chicken
1 can (11 oz.) Mandarin orange segments
1 red Delicious apple
1 cup green seedless grapes
1/3 cup mayonnaise
Dash of salt

Drain orange slices; place in a bowl. Dice apple; do not peel. Dip apple into liquid from orange segments (prevents browning); then drain and place in bowl with orange slices.

Combine other ingredients with the fruit. Toss lightly. Serve on lettuce cups. 4 servings.

Quick Chop Suey
Chow Mein Noodles or Rice
Vanilla Ice Cream with Apricots

Quick Chop Suey

1 1/4 pounds ground beef
4 stalks celery, sliced
1 large onion, diced
1 tablespoon oil
1 clove garlic, minced
1 tablespoon brown sugar
2 tablespoons soy sauce
2 tablespoons cornstarch
1 cup water
1/2 teaspoon salt, if desired
1/8 teaspoon pepper
1 1/2 cups fresh mung bean sprouts (or use canned)

Sauté the meat, celery, garlic, and onion until beef is light brown. Drain fat from the pan.

Dissolve cornstarch in water; then add soy sauce, sugar, salt, and pepper. Stir into the meat and vegetable mixture.

Add the mung beans; cover and cook until just tender.

Serve over rice or noodles.

Vanilla Ice Cream with Apricots

Vanilla ice cream
Chilled canned apricot halves

Dip ice cream into compotes. Top with apricot halves. Drizzle liquid from the apricots over and down the sides of the ice cream.

Roast Beef
Snow Peas and Mushrooms
Mexican Tomatoes
Crusty Whole-Wheat Bread
Vanilla Ice Cream with Raspberry Topping

This meal can be prepared in minutes.
Buy sliced roast beef at the deli or use planned-over roast.

Snow Peas and Mushrooms

2 cups fresh snow peas
1 cup sliced fresh mushrooms
3 or 4 green onions, sliced (or 1 small white)
1 or 2 tablespoons cooking oil
2 teaspoons soy sauce
1/4 cup water

Place oil in wok or frying pan; heat on medium-high. Add all the vegetables. Stir-fry 1 minute.

Reduce heat to medium and add soy sauce and water. Cook 1 or 2 more minutes. Serves 3 or 4.

Mexican Tomatoes

These tomatoes are hot but good. Reduce the amount of pepper for less seasoning.

2 tomatoes, peeled and sliced	**1/2 teaspoon salt**
2 green onions, sliced	**1/2 teaspoon sugar**
1 or 2 chili peppers, chopped	**3 tablespoons vinegar**
1/2 teaspoon basil	**1/3 cup salad oil**

Remove the seeds and membrane from the pepper (the *really* hot part).

Combine seasonings; stir to blend. Toss vegetables in the dressing. Serves 4.

Vanilla Ice Cream with Raspberry Topping

This is a quick, nutritious dessert.

Vanilla ice cream	**Frozen raspberries**

Defrost raspberries until nearly thawed. (They should still have ice crystals.)

Dip ice cream into serving dishes. Drizzle the thawed fruit and juice on top and down the sides of the ice cream.

"Better is bread with a happy heart than riches in vexation."
Amen-em-apt, 700 BC

"The less tenderness a man has in his nature, the more he requires of others."

Rahel

Baked Squash
Slaw
(see Index)
Cheese Muffins
(see Index)
Pumpkin Pie
or
Melon Wedge

This menu is a true vegetarian delight.

Baked Squash

1 zucchini squash, sliced
2 small yellow crookneck squash, sliced
1 tomato, sliced in circles
1 onion, sliced in rings
½ teaspoon soy sauce
Butter
¼ teaspoon salt
¼ teaspoon pepper
1 teaspoon basil
Cheddar cheese, grated

Butter a casserole dish. Place both squashes in bottom of container. Sprinkle soy sauce over squash.

Lay onion and tomatoes on top of squash. Sprinkle salt, pepper, and basil on top of vegetables. Top with grated cheese and dot with butter.

Bake in 375 °F. oven 25-30 minutes.

Pumpkin Pie

2 (16 oz.) cans pumpkin
1 (14 oz). can sweetened condensed milk
2 eggs
1/3 cup pecans, chopped
1/2 teaspoon mace
1 teaspoon cinnamon
1/2 teaspoon salt
3/4 teaspoon ginger

Beat eggs. Add milk, pumpkin, and spices; whip to blend. Fold in pecans and pour into one pie shell.

Bake 60-65 minutes—until knife comes out clean when inserted into pie.

"What is a home without a Bible?
'Tis a home where daily bread
For the body is provided,
But the soul is never fed."

Charles Meigs

"Room can always be found for a delicacy."

Babylonian Talmud, 450

Corned Beef and Cheese Sandwich
Cherry Tomatoes Broccoli Flowerets
Potato Chips
Blueberries and Cream

Corned Beef and Cheese Sandwich

Rye bread
Corned beef
Swiss cheese
Sliced canned mushrooms

For each sandwich, place corned beef on one slice of bread. Add the mushrooms and cheese. Top with another piece of bread.

Wrap with plastic wrap or waxed paper. Microwave 30-60 seconds—until cheese melts.

Note: No salad dressing is needed, but mustard could be used if desired.

Blueberries and Cream

1/3 cup fresh blueberries per serving
Whipped cream or topping

Wash and drain blueberries; chill. Place blueberries in a dessert dish. Top with a dollop of whipped cream.

It is oh-so-good and easy too!

Creamed Eggs with Ham

Raw Fresh Vegetables **Pickled Beets**

(Purchase)

Blackberry Doughnut

(see Index)

This is a quick brunch, lunch, or dinner menu.

Creamed Eggs with Ham

Sliced baked ham
Bread for toast
1 can (10 3/4 oz.) celery soup
1/2 can (soup) milk
1/2 teaspoon celery seed
Dash of cayenne pepper
1/4 teaspoon salt
2 tablespoons chopped parsley
3 or 4 hard-cooked eggs

Warm ham in bottom of pan; remove. Combine soup, milk, and seasonings in pan; bring to boiling point while stirring.

Slice whole eggs into eighths lengthwise. Add eggs to sauce; heat to warm eggs.

Toast bread; place on serving plate. Top each piece of toast with a ham slice. Pour creamed eggs over the ham and toast. Garnish with parsley and paprika. Serves 2.

Raw Fresh Vegetables

Broccoli
Cauliflower
Squash

Cut broccoli and cauliflower into flowerets. Slice squash into circles. Serve immediately or store covered with cold water.

To serve: Drain water and arrange attractively on a serving plate.

Cold Cuts
Marinated Artichoke Hearts
(Purchase)
Dilled Okra Pods and Brussels Sprouts
(Purchase)
Sliced Carrots and Squash
Candied Kumquats or Dates and Cookies
(Purchase)

Arrange the meat and cheese, vegetables, and pickles on a large serving tray along with lettuce and tomatoes. Set out mustard and mayonnaise and a selection of breads.

This noncook meal offers a beautiful, nutritious repast in almost any location—dining room, terrace, beach, etc.—wherever you desire.

Sliced Carrots and Squash

Carrots

Squash—yellow crookneck or zucchini

Wash squashes; slice into circles. Pare carrots; slice into narrow sticks. Serve immediately, or refrigerate in cold water.

Oriental Chicken Supreme
Artichoke Hearts and Green Beans
Cranberry Sauce Olives and Pickles
Hot Rolls
(Purchase)
Pears and Provolone Cheese

A simply delicious meal which is suitable for a special occasion, yet it can be prepared in 30 minutes.

Pears and Provolone Cheese

Fresh pears **Provolone cheese**

Set cheese out of refrigerator before preparing the meal. It improves in flavor if allowed to sit out 30-60 minutes before serving.

Serve unpeeled pears and the cheese attractively arranged on a tray for dessert.

Oriental Chicken Supreme

4 supremes (boned chicken breasts from 2 fryers)
2 tablespoons butter
1 tablespoon oil
2 cloves garlic, minced
1 tablespoon cornstarch
1 tablespoon brown sugar
1 1/2 teaspoons soy sauce
1/2 teaspoon ginger
1 can (15 1/2 oz.) chunk pineapple

Heat butter, oil, and garlic in frying pan. Sauté chicken breasts 3 or 4 minutes on each side; use medium-high heat. They should be lightly browned, but not totally done at this stage.

Remove from pan; set aside.

Make a sauce by combining in a small bowl cornstarch, brown sugar, soy sauce, and juice drained from the pineapple. Stir with a whisk to dissolve the ingredients. Add liquid to the frying pan. Cook on low heat, stirring often to make a sauce.

Place the chicken and pineapple chunks in the sauce; stir; cover. Heat on simmer 5-8 minutes. Serves 4. Garnish with parsley if desired.

Hint: Chicken will cook in less time if cut into one-inch strips.

Artichoke Hearts and Green Beans

1 can (8 1/2 oz.) artichoke hearts
1 can (16 oz.) green beans (Blue Lake whole beans)
Drained pimiento strips (optional)
1/4 cup butter
1 tablespoon lemon juice
1/3 teaspoon salt

Open cans of vegetables. Place vegetables in a container to warm; cover.

The vegetables may be heated in a microwave oven or on top of a range. If using a microwave, drain most of the liquid before warming. Heat on high (3-4 minutes) until warm. Drain liquid from vegetables.

Melt butter, add lemon juice, add salt. Add to drained vegetables. Toss gently. Serves 4.

Baked Ham
Braised Celery
or
Baked Sweet Potatoes
Pickled Peaches
(Purchase)
More than Cornbread
Ice Cream with Chocolate Topping

Purchase baked ham or use planned-over meat. Serve the pickled peaches chilled.

Braised Celery

4 stalks celery
1 tablespoon butter
Salt and pepper to taste

Slice celery diagonally. Place in 1/2 cup boiling water. Cover and cook 3-4 minutes. Drain; add seasonings. Celery should be crunchy. Serves 2.

Baked Sweet Potatoes

There are several types of sweet potatoes available. Some are mealy when cooked and others soft. The soft ones tend to be redder and sweeter. Either type can be baked and both are very nutritious.

I small sweet potato per serving

Wash the potatoes with a brush. Grease skins with margarine.

Bake in a 400° oven for 45 minutes.

or

Bake in microwave oven 5 minutes—turning halfway through cooking.

More than Cornbread

This bread is so light and airy it melts in the mouth. It truly is more than cornbread.

1 cup flour, sifted
1½ cups cornmeal
1 tablespoon sugar
½ teaspoon soda
1 teaspoon salt
1 package dry yeast
1 cup sour cream
1 cup buttermilk
2 eggs
½ cup margarine (1 stick), melted

Sift flour; combine with other dry ingredients, including the yeast; set aside.

Beat eggs; add sour cream, buttermilk, and melted margarine to the eggs.

Blend all ingredients together. Pour into 24 muffin cups. Bake 10-15 minutes at 450°. Extra muffins freeze well. If freezing, allow to cool; package, then freeze.

Chocolate Topping

1 teaspoon butter
½ cup white corn syrup
1½ tablespoons cocoa
⅓ teaspoon vanilla extract

Combine syrup and cocoa; stir to blend; then heat with butter just to boiling. Remove from heat; stir in vanilla.

Pour over ice cream. Add nuts if desired—not necessary.

Pans in an oven should never touch a wall or each other. Hot spots develop when pans touch.

When buying poultry, buy the larger bird for the highest ratio of meat to bone: i.e., a two-and-a-half-pound fryer has more meat than a two-pound fowl. Both have approximately the same amount of bone.

Soak fresh broccoli, cabbage, and cauliflower in cold salt water for five minutes to remove insects.

Peel onions under running water. You will have fewer tears.

Sliced Smoked Turkey
Celery with Blue Cheese
Pickled Heart of Artichokes
Tomato with Alfalfa Sprouts
Crackers or Whole Wheat Bread
Blueberry Trifle

This menu is delightful in warm weather. Serve the main course on individual plates. The colors are beautiful together on a plate, and there will be fewer dishes to wash.

Blueberry trifle is an elegant dessert which is fast and easy to prepare.

Celery with Blue Cheese

2 stalks celery

Wash celery. Remove top from each stalk; cut stalks into three-inch sections.

Using a knife, pile blue cheese mixture into center of stalks. Serves 2.

Blue Cheese Mixture

¼ cup mayonnaise
2 tablespoons blue cheese
1 teaspoon capers
Paprika

Combine mayonnaise, blue cheese, and capers. Fill celery stalks with mixture. Sprinkle paprika on top of filling. Serves 2.

Hint: This mixture keeps well in the refrigerator.

Grated onion can be added if one desires.

Pickled Heart of Artichokes

Purchase pickled artichokes. Serve chilled.

Tomato with Alfalfa Sprouts

1 large tomato
Alfalfa sprouts
Olives

Wash and slice tomatoes. Place two slices of tomato on each plate. Top each slice with alfalfa sprouts.

Set an olive in the center of each stack.

Hint: These look like beautiful flowers.

Blueberry Trifle

An elegance-with-ease dessert. Use a glass trifle dish or bowl for this dessert.

Fresh strawberries or blackberries may be substituted for blueberries if desired.

1 package ladyfingers
Blueberry jam or jelly (or substitute another jelly)
1 (5⅝ oz.) package vanilla pudding mix (not instant)
1 cup fresh blueberries

Split ladyfingers; cover tops and bottoms with jelly. Sandwich ladyfingers back together. Lightly butter inside of glass bowl. Cover bottom of the bowl with ladyfingers; then stand them up around the bowl. (The butter helps them stick to the side.)

Prepare pudding mixture, following package directions. Pour some of the pudding over the ladyfingers in the bottom of the bowl. Arrange a layer of fruit on top of the pudding. Repeat layers again. The top layers should be fruit.

Whipped cream may be added to top if desired.

"Dost thou love life? Then do not squander time, for that's the stuff life is made of."

Benjamin Franklin

"Time is what we want most, but what we use worst."

Penn

When buying food, compare cost per serving, not cost per pound—for example, how much does good quality beef cost with the bone in *vs*. boneless?

To separate uncooked bacon slices: Remove the bacon from the carton; then roll the inner packet up jellyroll fashion. The bacon slices will come apart.

Quick Pizza
Finger Vegetables
Sherbet

This informal, quick-cook meal can be prepared in 15 minutes.

Quick Pizza

2 English muffins
3 tablespoons barbecue sauce
½ teaspoon oregano (or basil) flakes
½ teaspoon parsley flakes
Mozzarella cheese (4 tablespoons grated or 4 slices)
Sliced pepperoni

Combine barbecue sauce and herb flakes.

Split muffins; spread cut sides with barbecue sauce mixture. Cover with cheese; then add sliced pepperoni.

Broil until cheese melts. Serves 2.

Hint: Add sliced olives to the top if desired.

Finger Vegetables

Fresh vegetables of your choice such as: cauliflower, broccoli, carrot, zucchini, yellow summer squash, celery, or radish.

Wash vegetables; carrots need to be peeled; other vegetables need not be peeled.

Slice or break vegetables into small portions (appropriate for eating with fingers).

Poached Trout
Tomato-Avocado-Watercress Salad
Pound Cake with Cherry Topping
French Bread

An elegance-with-ease meal.

Prepare the dessert and salad first. The fish cooks in four to seven minutes, so it is a good idea to have most other food prepared before the fish is placed into the poaching water.

Poached Trout

This fish is poached on top of the stove in a large covered pan such as a frying pan with lid.

It is a low-calorie, delicious protein food.

1 rainbow trout large enough to serve 2 people

Poaching Water

1 quart water
3 tablespoons vinegar
1 shallot or green onion
1/2 teaspoon salt
1/4 teaspoon dill weed
Peppercorns

Place all ingredients for the poaching water into a pan large enough to hold the fish. Bring to boil.

Add the fish; cover. Turn down the heat on the stove; the fish should not be boiled. Poach it at just below simmer 4-7 minutes. Do not overcook. It should be juicy, not dry and flaky.

Hint: If cooking more fish, increase the amount of poaching water used.

Tomato-Avocado-Watercress Salad

Slice tomato; place on bed of watercress on individual salad plate. Top with a large serving of avocado dressing.

Avocado Dressing

1/2 cup sour cream
1/2 large or 1 small avocado
1/4 cup salad oil
1 clove garlic
1/2 jalapeno pepper (remove seeds and white membrane)
2 tablespoons lemon juice

Peel avocado and remove the seed. Place all ingredients into the bowl of a food processor or blender. Pulse on and off to combine. Whip.

Hint: This dressing is also good as a dip with crackers, vegetables, and chips.

Pound Cake with Cherry Topping

Purchase pound cake. Place two slices on each dessert plate.

Dip warm cherry topping over the cake at serving time.

Cherry Topping

8 oz. cherries (frozen, pitted, unsweetened)
2 tablespoons water
1 tablespoon cornstarch
2 tablespoons water
1/4 cup sugar
1 tablespoon lemon juice

Place cherries and 2 tablespoons water into a small saucepan. Bring to boil; cook 1 minute.

In a cup combine the cornstarch, water, sugar, and lemon juice. Stir to dissolve the cornstarch and sugar in the liquid.

Add to the warm cherries. Stir and cook on low heat to form a sauce (approximately 1-2 minutes). Serves 2.

To remove burned-on stains from metal pans, add baking soda to water; boil several minutes.

To remove burned-on food from cast iron pans, boil vinegar and water in pan. Then wash, dry, and recoat with oil.

Wooden cutting boards and dishes should be washed in soapy water and wiped dry. If wood appears to be dry, rub with salad oil.

Wash enamel stove tops when cool; otherwise they will craze.

Crunchy Creamed Chicken in Patty Shells
Lettuce Wedge with Two Cheese
Salad Dressing
Cranberry Sauce Pickled Okra
Melon Slice of the Season

This is a simple-to-prepare meal which can be fixed in thirty minutes.

Purchase frozen patty shells. Put them in to bake first. They take approximately twenty-five minutes to bake.

Prepare the other food while the shells bake. If that is done, everything should be ready at the same time.

Crunchy Creamed Chicken in Patty Shells

- 1 can ($10\frac{1}{2}$ oz.) chicken mushroom soup
- $\frac{1}{2}$ can milk
- 1 clove garlic
- $\frac{1}{2}$ teaspoon Worcestershire sauce
- $\frac{1}{4}$ teaspoon crushed sage
- 1 can (5 oz.) chicken or $\frac{3}{4}$ cup diced cooked chicken
- 4 oz. sliced water chestnuts

Crush clove of garlic in a saucepan. Add the soup, milk, Worcestershire sauce, and sage. Bring to boil; then turn to low heat while stirring. Simmer one or two minutes.

Add the diced chicken and water chestnuts. Place patty shells on serving plate; fill with creamed chicken.

This will fill four shells.

Lettuce Wedge with Two Cheese Salad Dressing

Slice iceberg lettuce into moon-shaped wedges. Place one wedge on each salad plate.

Dip salad dressing over top of each wedge.

Two Cheese Salad Dressing

1 cup cottage cheese
1/4 cup blue cheese
1 clove garlic
Dash of salt and pepper

Place all ingredients into the bowl of a blender or food processor. Process until smooth.

Serve over salad greens. Sprinkle top of salad with paprika if desired.

Badly tarnished brass and copper can be cleaned with a paste of hot vinegar and salt. Rinse immediately since pitting could occur if salt were left on the metal.

A small, open container of baking soda in the refrigerator keeps it smelling fresh.

Tuna Bake
French Rolls
Baked Apples
(see Index)

This is an oven meal which uses only one dish for the main course. That reduces preparation and clean-up time immensely.

Tuna Bake

1 can (5 oz.) sliced water chestnuts, drained
1 (7 oz.) can tuna
1 cup cooked green peas
Chinese noodles or slightly crushed potato chips
Grated Cheddar cheese
1 can (10¾ oz.) cream of celery soup
⅓ cup milk
1 onion, diced
¼ teaspoon dill weed
Paprika

Combine soup, milk, onion, and dill in a 1-quart casserole. Add the tuna, water chestnuts, and peas.

Top with Chinese noodles or potato chips; then sprinkle with cheese. Shake on a little paprika.

Bake 30 minutes in a 350° oven.

Chicken Livers in Water Chestnut Sauce
Steamed Spinach
Golden Marshmallow Salad
Pumpkin Cornbread
(or purchase bread)

This unconventional meal is remarkably nutritious and tasty.

Chicken Livers in Water Chestnut Sauce

1 pound chicken livers
2 or 3 tablespoons oil for cooking
1/4 cup flour
1/2 teaspoon sage, crushed
1/2 teaspoon salt
1/2 teaspoon pepper
1 can (8 oz.) water chestnuts
1/2 cup evaporated milk
1 or 2 green onions, chopped

Rinse livers in cool water; drain. Remove any discolored tissue.

Combine flour, sage, salt, and pepper in a small bag. Toss the livers in the flour mixture long enough to coat.

Heat cooking oil in a frying pan over medium-high heat.

Shake the livers to remove excess flour. Sauté them 6-7 minutes, turning frequently. Remove from pan.

Add the onions, evaporated milk, and water chestnuts to the pan. Lower the heat; stir these ingredients while scraping the pan bottom.

When heated, pour over the livers. Serves 3 or 4.

Golden Marshmallow Salad

1 1/4 cups grated carrots
1 small can crushed pineapple
1/3 cup miniature marshmallows
3 tablespoons mayonnaise
2 tablespoons juice from canned pineapple
Dash salt

Drain juice from pineapple; set aside.

Combine the mayonnaise, two tablespoons pineapple juice, and salt; stir to blend.

Add the marshmallows, carrots, and pineapple. Toss to coat with dressing.

Serve from a bowl or in lettuce cups. This makes 4 servings.

Hint: Celery or raisins may be added if desired.

Pumpkin Cornbread

1 1/2 cups flour
1 1/4 cups yellow cornmeal
1/2 teaspoon soda
1/2 teaspoon mace
1 teaspoon cinnamon
1 tablespoon baking powder
1 1/2 teaspoons salt
1/3 cup butter
3 eggs
1 cup cooked pumpkin
1/2 can (16 oz.) whole berry cranberry sauce
2/3 cup chopped pecans

Sift flour; combine with meal, baking powder, salt, soda, mace, and cinnamon. Set dry ingredients aside.

In the bowl of a mixer or food processor (using dough blade) cream butter and eggs. Add the pumpkin and cranberry sauce.

Blend in the dry ingredients, then the pecans. Do not overblend.

Pour into a greased and floured pan—round 10 inch or one 9 x 5 loaf pan. Bake approximately 60 minutes.

Salmon Rarebit
Piquant Vegetables
Frozen Strawberry Topping on Pound Cake

Salmon Rarebit

Make up the salmon mixture. Toast bread; spread with salmon. Place on serving plate; pour cheese rarebit on top of salmon mixture. Serve immediately. This recipe serves 2.

Salmon Mixture

1 can (7¾ oz.) salmon, drained and bones removed
1 tablespoon mayonnaise
¼ teaspoon dill weed
½ cup diced celery
1 tablespoon chopped pickle
Dash of salt
Dash of pepper

Cheese Rarebit

1 (10¾ oz.) can Cheddar cheese soup
½ (soup) can milk
1 tablespoon lemon juice
Dash of red hot sauce
¼ teaspoon dill weed

Combine all ingredients while stirring over low heat. Bring to boil, but do not boil. Serve warm over salmon mixture and toast. Serves 2.

Piquant Vegetables

These vegetables can be served warm or cold for a salad. Either way the vegetables should be crunchy (barely cooked).

They keep several days if covered and refrigerated.

Piquant Seasonings

1 can tomato soup
1/2 cup salad oil
3/4 cup vinegar
1/4 cup brown sugar
1/4 teaspoon ginger

Combine ingredients; set aside.

Vegetables

1 medium onion, sliced into rings
1 green pepper, sliced into thin rings
2 cups diagonally sliced carrots
1 cup sliced mushrooms
1 1/2 cups cauliflower, broken into small flowers

Place vegetables into a container. Pour piquant seasonings over them; stir. Cover; cook 2 minutes in a microwave oven. Stir; cover and cook 2-3 more minutes. Serve warm or cold.

Frozen Strawberry Topping on Pound Cake

Frozen strawberries (or fresh)
Frozen pound cake
Frozen topping

Place 2 slices frozen pound cake on each individual dessert plate.

Partially thaw strawberries (they should still be icy).

Combine frozen topping and strawberries. Dip large servings on top of the cake.

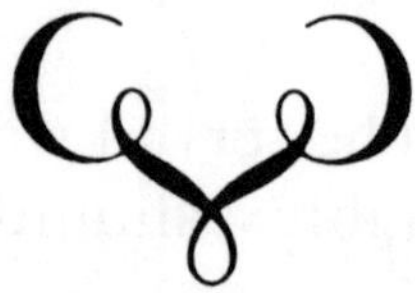

Limit cleanup when frosting cake. Place cake on rack; place rack over paper. Pour frosting over cake; let drip onto paper. Toss paper into garbage to clean up.

Remove fat from top of soup or stew in a hurry. Wrap ice cubes in a paper towel; run over top of food. Chilled fat will stick to the paper towel.

When broiling meat, turn it with tongs. Meat speared with a fork loses juices.

"Great is the meal which brings together people who are distant to each other."

Babylonian Talmud

Baked Chicken Drumettes

Baked Apples   Baked Pork and Beans

Jelled Strawberries and Cream

or

Ice Cream

This is a spicy, delicious oven meal. If you wish, add a green salad or sliced tomatoes and pickles to the menu.

Garlic bread (see Index) would be great with this meal.

Baked Chicken Drumettes

12 to 15 chicken drumettes (top of chicken wings)
2/3 cup barbecue sauce
1/4 cup water
1 clove garlic
1 small onion
1/4 cup raisins
1/2 teaspoon salt
1/4 teaspoon pepper

Place all of the ingredients except the chicken in a blender or food processor. Pulse on and off to dice and blend.

Place the drumettes one layer thick in a pan. Pour the sauce over the chicken; coat all the chicken with the sauce.

Bake in a 350° oven 45-50 minutes—until tender. Serves 4.

Hint: I spoon the sauce over the chicken, or turn them once during the cooking.

Baked Apples

4 baking apples
1 cup sugar
Cinnamon

Core the apples, removing all the seeds. If the apples are large, cut each one in half, forming rings.

Place in a baking dish. Pour water around them until it half covers the apples.

Pour the sugar into the center of each apple. Sprinkle cinnamon on top.

Bake uncovered until tender, approximately 45 minutes.

Baked Pork and Beans

1 can (16 oz.) pork and beans
1 or 2 tablespoons brown sugar
2 tablespoons barbecue sauce
2 teaspoons bacon drippings
1/4 teaspoon curry power
Dash of salt and pepper

Combine all ingredients.

Bake in 350° oven 30-45 minutes or in a microwave oven 4-8 minutes (until bubbling hot). Serves 3 or 4.

Jelled Strawberries and Cream

1 package (10 oz.) frozen strawberries
1 package (3 oz.) strawberry or cherry gelatin
1 cup water
1 1/2 cups vanilla ice cream

Heat water to boiling; add the gelatin and stir to dissolve.

Remove from heat and add frozen strawberries. Stir to defrost. Add the ice cream; stir to blend.

Pour into individual compotes or one glass bowl.

Place in the refrigerator until congealed—approximately 20 minutes.

Hint: This dish also can be served as a congealed salad—a sweet one.

Squash Omelet
Green Salad
Whole-Grained Bread
Angelfood Cake with Strawberries

Squash Omelet

1 cup sliced squash (zucchini or yellow)
1 green onion, chopped
1 tablespoon butter
1 tablespoon oil
3 or 4 eggs
1/4 cup Parmesan cheese, grated
Dash of salt
Dash of pepper

Beat eggs; add cheese, salt, and pepper; set aside.

Use a nonstick frying pan if you have one. Heat butter and oil. Sauté zucchini and onion 4-6 minutes. Turn heat to low.

Pour the egg-cheese mixture over vegetables in the pan. Cook to set eggs. Serves 2.

Green Salad

Lettuce
Bell pepper
Green onion
Avocado salad dressing (see Index)
(or purchase dressing)

Shred lettuce; toss with sliced pepper and onion. Top with avocado salad dressing.

Angelfood Cake with Strawberries

Angelfood cake
Strawberries
Whipped cream or topping

Place one slice of cake on each individual dessert plate. Top with 1/3 cup sliced strawberries and a dollop of whipped cream.

"Simplicity, simplicity, simplicity! I say, let your affairs be as two or three, and not a hundred or a thousand."

Thoreau

"For never anything can be amiss
When simpleness and duty tender it."

Shakespeare, *A Midsummer-Night's Dream*

Speedy Chicken Soup
Banana-Bean Sprout Salad
Crescent Sweet Rolls

Speedy Chicken Soup

1 package (3 oz.) ramen noodles with chicken flavor
2½ cups water or chicken broth
1 can (10¾ oz.) chicken mushroom soup

Combine water and chicken mushroom soup; bring to boil while stirring.

Add the ramen noodles and the contents of the seasoning packet (which comes with the noodles). Cook 2 or 3 minutes. Serves 2-3.

Hint: I prefer to use less than the full package of seasoning.

Banana-Bean Sprout Salad

Banana
Peanut butter
Alfalfa bean sprouts

Arrange on each individual salad plate a bed of alfalfa sprouts.

Slice a banana into circles; arrange on top of the bean sprouts. Add a dollop of peanut butter on top of each salad.

Crescent Sweet Rolls

These luscious rolls are good for dessert and breakfast sweet rolls, and they are ideal for coffee get-togethers.

They can be prepared and baked in twenty minutes. Serve warm.

1 can (8 oz.) crescent rolls
3 tablespoons sugar
1 teaspoon cinnamon
1 teaspoon nutmeg
3 tablespoons raisins
32 miniature marshmallows

Preheat oven to 375°F.

Open can; separate dough into 8 rolls. Combine sugar, cinnamon, nutmeg. Sprinkle all over the inside surface of each roll. (Use about 1 teaspoon per roll.)

Dot inside of rolls with raisins.

Place 4 marshmallows on large end of each roll. Starting at the big end, roll up each roll. Pinch the sides, totally encasing the marshmallows.

Sprinkle leftover sugar mixture on top of rolls.

Bake 12-14 minutes on an aluminum foil-covered cookie sheet.

Creamed Salmon
Savory Broccoli
Honeydew with Fruit

Creamed Salmon

1 can (5½ oz.) salmon
1 can (10½ oz.) mushroom soup
½ can liquid (combine liquid from the salmon and milk to make ½ can)
1 teaspoon dried onion flakes
¼ teaspoon dill weed or tarragon
1 small can mushrooms, drained
Dash of salt and pepper

Combine mushroom soup, liquid, onion flakes, dill, salt, and pepper in a saucepan. Bring to boil while stirring.

Add the mushrooms and salmon. Heat just enough to warm.

Serve over English muffins or toast, or in pastry cups. Serves 2.

Savory Broccoli

1 (10 oz.) package frozen broccoli (or 1 pound fresh broccoli)
1 tablespoon lemon juice
1 tablespoon butter
½ tablespoon soy sauce
¼ teaspoon dry mustard
½ tablespoon seeds (sesame or carraway)

Cook broccoli in boiling water until crisp tender (5 or 6 minutes).

or

Place broccoli into a microwave in a 1-quart container with 1/4 cup water. Frozen broccoli should be cooked icy side up.

Cover the container; cook 3 minutes. Remove from oven; stir. Cook 3-4 more minutes.

Drain the broccoli and place on a serving dish. Drizzle hot seasonings over the top, coating well.

The seasonings can be heated 25 seconds in a microwave, or to bubbling in a small saucepan. Serves 3 or 4.

Honeydew with Fruit

Honeydew melon
Fresh strawberries or blueberries
Banana

Chill melon and berries.

Cut the melon into circles; remove rind.

Place one circle on each individual serving plate.

Slice banana into circles. Combine with berries and pile into center of melon slices.

Top with sherbet or drizzle salad dressing over the top.

Hint: A sprig of mint would be nice for color.

Parmesan Chicken Breasts
Minted Peas and Mushrooms
Garlic Bread
Raspberry Peach

Parmesan Chicken Breasts

Boned chicken breasts from 2 fryers
2 tablespoons cooking oil
2 tablespoons butter or margarine
1/3 cup flour
1/2 teaspoon salt
1/4 teaspoon celery seed
1 tablespoon chopped parsley
3 tablespoons lemon juice
2 tablespoons Parmesan cheese

Cut chicken breasts into one-inch strips. Combine flour, salt, celery seed, and parsley. Dredge chicken with seasoned flour mixture.

Heat butter and oil over medium-high heat. Sauté meat until lightly browned on sides (5 to 8 minutes). Remove chicken to a heatproof platter.

Pour lemon juice into pan. Stir the juice and scrape the pan to blend flavors; pour over the meat.

Sprinkle meat with Parmesan cheese. Run under the broiler long enough to just heat the cheese. Serves 4.

Minted Peas and Mushrooms

1 (10 oz.) package frozen green peas
1 (6 oz.) can mushrooms, drained
Dash salt
Dash pepper
½ tablespoon butter
1 teaspoon lemon juice
2 teaspoons chopped mint leaves or 1 tablespoon dry mint

Cook peas following package directions. When nearly done, add the drained mushrooms. Continue cooking until mushrooms are heated.

Drain most of the liquid from the vegetables. Add the seasonings; toss gently to blend flavors. Serves 4.

Garlic Bread

1 loaf French or Italian bread
2 tablespoons butter
1 or 2 cloves garlic, crushed

Slice bread diagonally, being careful not to cut through the bottom crust.

Melt butter; add crushed garlic. Brush the garlic butter between each slice and on top of the bread.

Wrap in aluminum foil around the bread. Heat in a 350° oven 15 minutes.

Hint: If you want just one or two slices of garlic bread, slice the bread and put it on aluminum foil. Brush top of bread with garlic butter and toast under the broiler.

Raspberry Peach

¼ cup raspberry jam
1 tablespoon lemon juice
4 peach halves

Combine juice and jam; heat to melt jam.

Place one peach half into individual compotes. Pour warm jam mixture over the peaches.

If desired, top with whipped cream or topping. Serves 4.

Mexican Salad Dinner
Honey Nut Spice Cake
(or purchase dessert)

This salad is a meal in a bowl, and there is nothing to cook.

Mexican Salad Dinner

1/2 head iceberg lettuce or mixed salad greens
1 (16 oz.) can garbanzo beans
2 tomatoes
1 small bell pepper
2 green onions
1 (6 1/2 oz.) can tunafish
Corn chips
3/4 cup grated Cheddar cheese
Avocado dressing

Open can of beans; drain and discard liquid. Cut tomatoes into wedges; chop onions and peppers. Break lettuce into bite-size pieces.

Toss all the vegetables, corn chips, and drained tunafish gently to mix in a salad bowl.

Sprinkle grated cheese on top of the salad.

Pour the avocado dressing on top of the salad, or serve it in a side dish.

Avocado-Cheese Dressing

1/3 cup ricotta cheese
Salad oil
2 tablespoons lemon juice
1/2 jalapeno pepper (remove membrane and seeds)
1 small avocado
1 clove garlic
1/4 teaspoon salt

Peel and seed the avocado. Place all the ingredients into the bowl of a food processor or blender. Pulse on and off to combine. Whip.

Honey Nut Spice Cake

Bake a spice cake in a 7 x 13-inch pan. Spread with icing.

Icing

3/4 cup crunchy peanut butter
1/2 cup honey
1/4 cup flaked coconut
2 tablespoons butter

Whip peanut butter, honey, and butter to combine.
Spread on top of cake. Sprinkle coconut on top.
If desired, the cake may be heated under a broiler just before serving.

"It is part of a wise man to feed himself with moderate pleasant food."

Spinoza

Broiled Chicken Breasts
Broiled Yellow Squash
Green Beans with Mixed Seasonings
Fruit Compote

Rolls or biscuits taste good with this colorful, delicious meal.

Green Beans with Mixed Seasonings

1 can (16 oz.) green beans

Open can; place beans and liquid in bottom of broiler pan. Spread beans out for even distribution.

No seasonings are added to the beans because the mixed seasonings from the chicken and squash are ample.

Place broiler rack over the beans. Follow directions for broiled chicken.

Broiled Chicken Breasts

4 chicken breasts (bone in)
1/3 cup margarine or butter
1 tablespoon lemon juice
1/2 teaspoon vegetable salt (celery or onion)
1/2 teaspoon sage

Rinse and drain chicken breasts. Place on broiler rack skin side down. Melt margarine in small container; add lemon juice and seasonings.

Brush butter mixture over rib side of the chicken breasts. Broil 5 inches from heat 10-15 minutes—until golden color.

Turn breasts skin side up. Brush that side with fat-seasonings mixture. Broil approximately 15 minutes on the second side—until done. Serves 4.

Broiled Yellow Squash

4 small (3-4 inch) yellow squash
1-1½ tablespoons butter or margarine
Dash paprika
Parmesan cheese
Dash salt

Squash should be young and tender for top flavor and texture.

Wash squash. Cook whole in boiling, salted water (4-6 minutes) until tender when pricked with a fork.

Drain water. Slice squash lengthwise. Place on broiler rack, cut side up.

Melt butter; pour over squash. Sprinkle cut sides with salt, paprika, and Parmesan cheese. Broil 2 minutes. Serves 4.

Hint: The squash can be boiled ahead of time—even the day before. Drain it; leave whole and store in the refrigerator until needed.

Slice, season, and broil when preparing meal.

Fruit Compote

1 can (11 oz.) Mandarin orange segments
2 Delicious apples
1 banana

Open can of orange segments; pour contents into a bowl.

Remove stem and seed from apples; do not peel. Chop into bite-size pieces; add to bowl.

Slice banana; add to bowl. Toss fruits gently. Serve in glass compotes—with plain cookies if desired.

Steamed Fish Fillet
Vegetable Medley
Banana Muffins
(or purchase bread)
Raspberry-Topped Pineapple

Banana muffins are included with this menu because they are so good, not because they are a quick-cook food.

The muffins freeze well and are an ideal food to prepare ahead and freeze for use on a busy day.

The other foods on this menu are fresh, savory, and quick cook.

Steamed Fish Fillet

When fish is steamed, it is not submerged in water but cooked in herb-laden steam.

Most people are acquainted with steamed vegetables, but not fish. Yet thin fish fillets can be steamed as well as poached, baked, or broiled. The fish remains tender, and there is no need to turn it over during cooking.

A pan used to steam vegetables is an ideal utensil to steam two or three servings of fish.

Place in Bottom of Steamer Pan

2 cups water
1 tablespoon tarragon
1 tablespoon dill weed
½ onion, chopped

Place Rack Over the Liquid

Cut one fish fillet (red snapper or salmon) into 3 or 4 strips.

Lay the fish, skin down, on the rack which is just above water level.

Sprinkle on Top of Fish

1 tablespoon lemon juice
½ onion, chopped
¼ teaspoon dill weed
Dash of salt
Dash of paprika

Cover the pan and bring water to boil. Steam 5-6 minutes over bubbling water.

The fish is done when the translucent flesh turns opaque. Do not overcook. Serves 2.

Vegetable Medley

2 or 3 carrots sliced thin
1 or 2 zucchini, sliced thin
1 onion sliced into circles
3 or 4 tablespoons cooking oil
¼ cup chopped parsley
Salt and pepper

Heat oil in a frying pan over medium-high heat. Stir-fry 4 or 5 minutes. Add the parsley, salt, and pepper. Cook, stirring often until the vegetables are done but still crunchy—approximately 1 or 2 more minutes.

Hint: Place the cooked fish in the center of a platter. Surround the fish with the colorful vegetables. This makes a beautiful serving plate.

Raspberry-Topped Pineapple

This is a beautiful, elegant-looking dessert.

1/2 fresh pineapple (or use canned spears)
Frozen raspberries

Slice pineapple lengthwise, then into quarters.

Using a knife, cut the pineapple along the shell to loosen. Cut into bite-size pieces. Leave cut pineapple in the shell.

Place one sectioned shell on each individual dessert plate.

Partially defrost raspberries; pour over pineapple.

Banana Muffins

2 cups flour
1 teaspoon soda
1 teaspoon baking powder
1/2 teaspoon cloves
1/2 teaspoon mace
1/2 teaspoon cinnamon
1/4 teaspoon salt
1 cup brown sugar
1/2 cup butter
2 eggs
1 large or 2 small ripe bananas
1 1/2 cups *cooked* brown rice
1/3 cup nuts

Sift flour, soda, baking powder, cloves, mace, cinnamon, and salt together; set aside.

Measure brown sugar, pressing to fill cup. Place sugar into the bowl of a food processor with metal blade (or use mixer).

Add butter; whip. Add eggs and sliced bananas. Pulse on and off to mash and blend. Dry ingredients are combined next. Last, add the nuts and rice. Pulse on and off to blend.

Bake in a 350° oven 40-50 minutes. Makes 18 muffins.

Hint: If using a mixer instead of a food processor, chop the nuts and slightly mash the bananas before adding to the mixture.

Melon-Ham-Cheese Salad
Cinnamon Sticks
Lime Sherbet

This festive salad plate is ideal for a hot day. It is both picturesque and cooling.

Apricot muffins or zucchini-carrot bread (both listed in the Index) would also be delicious with this meal.

Melon-Ham-Cheese Salad

1 cantaloupe
Berries (blueberries, strawberries, raspberries, or blackberries)
2 cups watermelon balls
12 baked ham slices
Cheddar cheese cut into 12 finger-length strips

Cut cantaloupe into 4 wedges. Remove membrane and seeds.

Using a melon ball scoop or a measuring spoon, cut out 3 melon balls down both sides of cantaloupe wedges.

Fill holes in cantaloupe with watermelon balls.

Combine extra watermelon and cantaloupe balls with the berries. Pile in the center of each cantaloupe wedge.

Wrap one slice ham around each piece of cheese; secure

with a toothpick. Attach—standing up—to top of fruit in a festive manner.

Garnish with mint. Serves 4.

Cinnamon Sticks

1 can (11 oz.) refrigerated soft breadsticks
4 tablespoons butter
4 tablespoons brown sugar
1 teaspoon cinnamon
Candied cherries
½ cup chopped pecans

Preheat oven to 350°F.

Melt butter in 2 cake pans. Add brown sugar and cinnamon to butter. Stir to blend.

Open can of bread sticks. Unroll dough and pull to stretch. Divide dough into 2 sections.

Starting in the center of each pan, spiral dough into a pinwheel. Drop nuts and cherries on top. Use fingers to punch nuts and fruit into the dough, and slightly spread the elastic mass.

Bake until golden brown.

Invert on serving plate.

"There is a majesty in simplicity."

Pope

"In character, in manners, in style, in all things, the supreme excellence is simplicity."

Longfellow

2

Brown Bagging

What to pack for lunch tomorrow? Just thinking about it seems a chore if you do it regularly.

There is no need to suffer brown-bag-boredom or choke on another dry sandwich! Relax and read on to discover a multitude of ideas, menus, and recipes for preparing luscious sack lunches.

People who regularly brown-bag-it are usually interested in saving time, money, and eating nutritious food not available in fast-food establishments.

It is a challenge to come up with interesting, good, and good-for-you food which can be fixed fast.

Plenty of these brown-bagging menus would be equally good for school lunches, picnics, hikes, and cycling trips. Most of the time you could use the same food, but alter how and where it is eaten.

A picnic can be elaborate or simple depending on how and where you serve it.

A lightweight backpack is recommended for hiking or biking. Pack it with nonspoilable foods.

The Art of Brown Bagging

Save time. 1. When making sandwiches, make several at the same time. There will be only one time for preparation and cleanup.

Freeze the extra sandwiches. Whoever needs a sandwich for lunch can grab one in the morning and stick it in his lunch sack. It will be thawed (but still cool) at lunchtime.

All frozen foods should be wrapped in moisture-vapor-proof wrappings.

Mayonnaise and salad dressing do not freeze well. If sandwiches are to be kept several days or weeks, spread both slices of bread with margarine or butter. This will prevent bread from becoming soggy from moisture in the filling.

Cream cheese and mustard can also be used for sandwich spreads since they freeze well.

2. Have you thought of freezing small cans of fruit or vegetable juice? It will thaw by lunch, yet still be cool. Also, it will keep a small lunch pack cool.

3. Freeze individual servings of chicken. It too will thaw by lunch. A drumstick, fresh raw vegetable, a roll, and beverage would make a delightful alternative to a sandwich.

4. Keep cookies, fruit, cake, etc., frozen in individual serving portions. They too are easy to drop into a bag in a hurry.

5. Cut food such as vegetables and fruits (unless you want a whole one) into bite-size pieces. Later they can be easily eaten with the fingers.

6. Next time you have soup or chili, freeze the leftovers. Freeze in small cartons or ice cube trays for individual servings. In the morning, heat the soup (microwave is fastest), and pour into a thermos.

Cold Food Cold and Hot Food Hot

Keep cold food cold and hot food hot to prevent bacterial growth. Pack cold food directly from the freezer or refrigerator into thermos or cold chest unless it is something that needs to thaw.

If you want a thermos to remain cold, try chilling it with ice water before filling.

When carrying hot foods, put hot water into the thermos a few minutes to preheat it.

People who regularly carry lunch will find a small widemouth thermos a good investment. It is great for soup, salad, fruit mixtures, meat and cheese spreads, etc.

Small insulated bags are useful for the regular lunch bag carrier.

Tuna in a Pocket
Fresh Plums
Beverage

This pocket sandwich gives you a meat and two vegetables plus bread. Add a beverage and fruit for a complete meal.

Tuna in a Pocket

1 can (6½ oz.) tuna
2 stalks celery, diced
1 tablespoon pickle relish or chopped pickle
2 tablespoons mayonnaise
1 teaspoon lemon juice
½ teaspoon dill weed
Dash salt and pepper
1 large pita bread round
Alfalfa sprouts

Combine all ingredients except alfalfa sprouts and bread.

Cut pita bread in half, forming two pockets. Stuff each pocket with tuna mixture. Top with alfalfa sprouts.

Hints:
1. Small canned shrimp may be substituted for the tuna.
2. Pocket bread is also called pita bread.

Tomato Soup
Anchovy-Cream Cheese Sandwich
Cookies or Fruit

The anchovy-cream cheese spread freezes beautifully. You'll want to keep a supply in the freezer.

I usually make triple-decker sandwiches with this spread, using both whole-wheat and white breads. The taste is interesting and rich—one-half sandwich might be enough for one person.

Anchovy-Cream Cheese Spread

8 oz. cream cheese
1 (2 oz.) can anchovies
½ small onion
3 tablespoons lemon juice
½ tablespoon dill weed
1 tablespoon mayonnaise
Milk, if needed

Open and drain oil from anchovies; place in food processor or blender. Put cheese and other ingredients into container.

Whip until fairly smooth, scraping sides as needed. Add a small amount of milk if too thick.

Smoked Turkey Sandwich
Tangy Carrot Toss
Cake

Pick up some smoked turkey at the deli. The meat and pumpernickel or whole-wheat bread spread with mustard make a delicious sandwich. Make several at one time if you desire; they freeze beautifully.

Tangy Carrot Toss

3 carrots, grated coarsely
4 slices canned pineapple, diced
1/2 cup dates, diced
1 tablespoon pineapple juice
1/2 tablespoon sugar
3 tablespoons yogurt

Combine ingredients. Chill. Serves 4.

Egg Salad Sandwich in French Roll
Cherry Tomatoes
Oatmeal Cookies
Beverage

Egg Salad Sandwich

3 hard-cooked eggs
1 large stalk celery
½ teaspoon basil
Dash salt
2 tablespoons mayonnaise
2 tablespoons pickle relish or chopped pickle
1 teaspoon prepared mustard

Wash celery; chop. Peel and chop eggs. Blend all ingredients. Keep refrigerated.

When making sandwich, split roll lengthwise—not all the way through. Fill with egg mixture.

"Nothing comes out of a sack but what was in it."
C. H. Spurgeon, 1869

Chicken in a Pocket
Raw Vegetable
Orange
Beverage

A raw vegetable, for example, sliced zucchini or yellow summer squash, would be a good accompaniment with this meal.

Chicken in a Pocket

1 round pita bread
3/4 cup cooked chicken
1 hard-boiled egg
1 large stalk celery
1/4 teaspoon onion salt
2 tablespoons sweet pickle relish or chopped olives
2 tablespoons mayonnaise

Dice chicken, egg, and celery; combine with other ingredients.

Cut pita bread in half; line with lettuce leaf. Stuff with chicken mixture. Serves 2.

Roast Beef Sandwich
Carrot-Apple-Raisin Salad
Milk

Carrot-Apple-Raisin Salad

1 carrot, diced or shredded
1 large apple
1/4 cup raisins
1 tablespoon mayonnaise

Leave peeling on apple; remove seeds and core; chop.

Toss all ingredients together. Keep refrigerated.

Serve on lettuce cup if serving on plate—otherwise from a bowl. Serves 2.

Hint: Add 2 tablespoons nuts if desired.

"Those who make the worst use of their time most complain of its shortness."

La Bruyere

"The first indication of domestic happiness is the love of one's home."

Montlosier

Pimento Cheese Sandwich
Coleslaw
Chocolate Pudding

With a food processor this cheese spread can be made in seconds. It will keep several days in the refrigerator.

Pimento Cheese Sandwich

1/2 pound Cheddar cheese
1/2 small onion
1 (4 oz.) jar pimento
3 tablespoons mayonnaise
1/4 teaspoon celery seeds
Dash salt, if desired

If you have a food processor, grate the cheese. Add metal blade and all ingredients. Process until just blended.

If not using a processor, grate the cheese and onion; combine with other ingredients. Store in refrigerator.

Nothing is more simple than greatness; indeed, to be simple is to be great.

Emerson

Ham Sandwich

Lettuce Tomato

Apple

Sugar Wafers

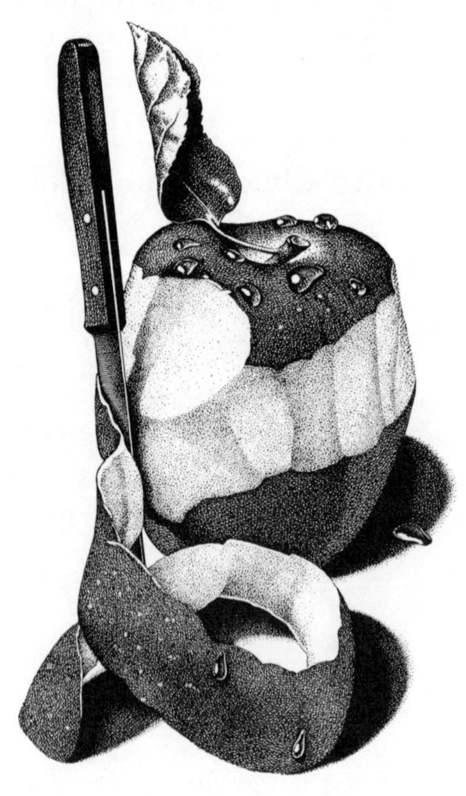

Non-Sandwich Ham and Cheese Date Rolls
Crackers
Milk
Vanilla Pudding

Try these non-sandwiches for a change in menu. They are especially tasty with whole grain crackers.

The sandwiches are also very good finger food for a party.

Ham and Cheese Date Rolls

Dates, pitted
Ham, sliced thin
Cream cheese, thinned with milk

Cut ham into one-inch strips.

Stuff dates with cream cheese.

Roll up each date with a ham strip. Secure with toothpick.

These freeze well, so make a lot at one time, saving yourself time.

Chili Bean Soup
Sliced Cheese
Crackers
Apricots
Beverage

A super-speedy meal. Just warm the soup and pour into a thermos. The other foods can be hurriedly dropped into a bag.

All cheeses have better flavor if served at room temperature—except cream and cottage. To bring out cheese flavor, let cheeses sit at room temperature 20-60 minutes before eating.

"The discovery of a new dish does more for happiness of man than the discovery of a star."

Brillant-Savarin

Tomato Juice
Deviled Ham-Egg Sandwich
Potato Chips
Fresh Plums

For a change, try this ham-egg mixture on pumpernickel bread.

The small can of juice, potato chips, and fruit could be placed in a bag as you go out the door.

Deviled Ham-Egg Sandwich

- 1 can (4½ oz.) deviled ham
- 1 hard-boiled egg
- 1 stalk celery
- ½ teaspoon prepared mustard
- Dash salt
- Dash pepper
- 2 or 3 tablespoons mayonnaise

Wash celery; chop.

Peel egg; chop.

Combine all ingredients.

Store in refrigerator. This does not freeze well because of the egg.

Vegetable Juice
Mixed Cheese Spread
Crackers
Pear

No time to make a sandwich? If you have this spread in the refrigerator, put some into a small container and take it along. Add some crackers, fresh fruit, and vegetable juice for a nutritious meal in minutes.

Mixed Cheese Spread

8 oz. cottage cheese
3 oz. sharp Cheddar cheese
Dash Worcestershire sauce
Dash red hot sauce
½ teaspoon dill weed

Use food processor or blender. Place all ingredients into bowl. Blend until smooth.

Use for sandwiches or as a spread on crackers.

It also is good party fare.

Hard Cooked Egg
Cherry Tomatoes or Can of Tomato Juice
Crackers
Grapes

Deviled Ham-Cream Cheese Sandwich
Celery Sticks
Apple
Lemonade

Try this sandwich spread on cracked wheat bread for a change.

Deviled Ham-Cream Cheese Sandwich

1 can (4½ oz.) deviled ham
1 (3 oz.) pkg. cream cheese
1 tablespoon onion
1 or 2 tablespoons mayonnaise

Place all ingredients into a blender or food processor. Pulse on and off to combine.

Spread on bread or crackers.

This mixture freezes beautifully.

Celery Sticks

Wash celery. Remove tops and bottom of each stalk. Slice into long thin slices. Eat, or store covered with cold water in the refrigerator.

No-Bread Lunch Roll
Crisp Nut Bars
Beverage

This is a no-cook, little preparation meal. Prepare the dessert at your leisure; it keeps well in the refrigerator or freezer.

The lunch roll is very low in calories since it has neither bread nor sandwich spread.

No-Bread Lunch Roll

Lettuce leaf for each serving
Sliced ham or chicken
Whole dill pickle

Place meat on lettuce leaf. Set pickle near the edge of leaf; roll up jellyroll fashion. Skewer with toothpick. Eat holding like a hot dog.

Crisp Nut Bars

1/4 cup honey
1/4 cup peanut butter
1/3 cup dry milk powder
1/3 cup raisins or diced dried fruit
2 cups crisp rice cereal
1/2 teaspoon vanilla

Place all ingredients into food processor bowl. Pulse on and off to blend.

If you do not own a processor, crush the cereal with a rolling pin; then combine ingredients.

Press into buttered square cake pan. Cut into bars. Refrigerates well.

When measuring honey or molasses, lightly grease the cup. They will stick less.

Honey which has crystallized will return to liquid if heated.

To get gelatin in a hurry, use a thin metal mold. Set mold in pan of ice water until firm (about one hour).

A tablespoon of coffee added to gravy or pan drippings gives color and flavor.

High temperature toughens meat, so always cook on as low a temperature as time and recipe allow.

3
Fast Breakfast

Nutritious, delicious food for breakfast doesn't have to take a long time to prepare. Neither does it have to be the traditional breakfast.

All you need for a complete breakfast is: a source of protein (egg, cheese, milk, meat, or peanut butter, for example); a fruit or vegetable; and bread or cereal.

Most nutritionists recommend that people eat one fourth of their daily calories at breakfast.

If schedules limit time, how about preparing something the night before? Whoever needs it can eat it in a rush or grab it as they go out the door.

It is generally accepted that approximately twelve million Americans do not eat breakfast.

Some of these people eat food later in the morning. Unfortunately, this food is frequently high in sugar and fat and low in nutrients.

The fast-paced lives individuals live often make them feel they need sleep more than food. Other people just aren't hungry in the morning. Some do not eat the meal because they want to lose weight and think it is a good way to do it. In fact, it is a very poor way to lower food intake. Late-morning hunger can lead to depression and overeating at lunch.

Many people skip breakfast because they don't feel like "cooking" when they are rushed. Some just do not like the traditional breakfast.

Food for Grazers

Breakfast is the one meal during which families find it the most difficult to sit down together. Even singles living alone seem to have little time to sit down for the meal.

What you eat is more important than how you eat it and where it is eaten. A new word has entered our vocabulary which describes how we frequently eat breakfast—grazing.

A lot of foods are easily portable. I call these take-along breakfast food. All you have to do is wrap them up or put them into a thermos and take them with you.

They are ideal for eating while waiting for the bus or at one's morning break.

"Life, within doors, has few pleasanter prospects than a neatly arranged and well-provisioned breakfast-table."

Nathaniel Hawthorne

Take-Along Breakfasts

Peanut Butter Balls

This is a good prepare-ahead and take-along food.

It is similar to a rich bowl of cereal—milk, cereal, and fruit—plus peanut butter and honey.

It tastes like candy and is a great snack.

1 cup bran flake cereal
1/2 cup dried apricots
1/2 cup dry milk powder
1/2 cup peanut butter
1/4 cup honey

Crush half of the cereal in food processor, blender, or with rolling pin. Set it aside in a small bag (plastic or paper).

Place apricots in food processor or blender; chop. Add milk powder, honey, and remaining cereal. Pulse on and off to blend, scraping sides of container.

Using your hands, roll into small bite-size balls.

Drop balls into sack containing crushed cereal. Toss lightly to coat balls with cereal.

Store in refrigerator or freezer.

"And then to breakfast with
What appetite you have."

William Shakespeare, *King Henry VIII*

Banana on a Stick

Prepare this eat-on-the-run breakfast ahead of time. Take it with you as you go.

1 banana per serving
Wheat germ
Yogurt
Wooden stick for pops

Peel banana. Insert stick into end of banana. Dip banana into yogurt; sprinkle with wheat germ. Freeze.

Banana Freeze

Banana freeze is a breeze. Prepare anytime; keep in the freezer. Good for breakfast, snacks, or a low-calorie dessert.

1 banana
Wooden pop sticks
1¼ cups orange juice
Paper cups

Peel; slice banana into blender bowl. Pour juice into blender. Whip until fairly smooth. Pour into paper cups or frozen pop containers. Insert wooden pop sticks. Freeze. Eat like a frozen ice cream pop.

Breakfast in a Pocket

Stuff the fruit-cheese mixture into the pocket bread; wrap it up; and away you go!

Pocket bread (also called pita bread)
½ cup cottage cheese, drained
½ canned peach, diced
Dash of mace

Cut bread into half. Use one-half per sandwich. Combine cheese, peach, and mace; stuff into pocket. Serves 1.

Apricot Bagel

1 bagel per serving
2 teaspoons apricot preserves per serving
2 teaspoons cream cheese per serving

Split bagel in half horizontally. Spread one cut side with cream cheese and the other side with apricot preserves. Put back together to form sandwich.

Hint: 1. Substitute English muffin if desired. 2. According to your time and taste, the bread might be toasted before adding the spread.

Peanut Butter Bagel

1 bagel per serving
2 tablespoons peanut butter (crunchy is better)

Follow directions for Apricot Bagel.

Ambrosia Cup

1 orange
1 apple
1 banana, sliced into circles
Small bunch of grapes (seedless or seeds removed)

Remove skin from orange. Cut orange into bite-size chunks, removing seeds.

Cut apple into bite-size chunks; remove seeds, but leave the skin.

Add banana and grapes. Toss lightly.

Put into a thermos or throw-away container to take along.

Graham Cracker Peanut Butter Sandwich

2 graham crackers per sandwich **Peanut butter**

Spread peanut butter on one cracker; top with other cracker. Wrap and take along.

Hint: Drink a glass of citrus juice or milk with this and you will have a complete meal.

Blueberry-Cheese Salad

½ cup cottage cheese **⅓ cup blueberries**

Toss lightly. Put into thermos; take it along.

Hint: You might eat whole-wheat crackers with this breakfast dish to have a complete meal.

Other Quick Take-Along Food Ideas

1. Apple with a Slice of Cheese
2. Banana and Milk
3. Cottage Cheese with Diced Cantaloupe

Blender Breakfasts

The blender is the ideal appliance to whip up a fast breakfast beverage.

High-Vitamin Breakfast Drink

1/4 cup dry milk powder
1/2 cup unsweetened pineapple juice
1/2 cup carrot juice
1/2 tablespoon honey

Place ingredients in blender; whip. Serve cold. 1 serving.

Strawberry Shake

3/4 cup skim milk
1/3 cup strawberries, fresh or frozen
1/4 teaspoon vanilla extract
Strawberry ice cream

Place a small scoop of ice cream, strawberries, and vanilla extract in blender. Whip.

Pour into tall glass, not filling the glass. Top with scoop of ice cream.

Double Milk Strawberry Shake

1/2 cup strawberries (fresh or frozen)
2/3 cup milk (skim or whole)
3 tablespoons skim milk powder
1/4 teaspoon vanilla extract
2 teaspoons sugar if using fresh berries
Strawberry ice cream

Combine all ingredients except ice cream in blender. Whip until serving consistency. Pour into tall glass; top with scoop of ice cream. Serves 1.

Hint: The extra milk powder doubles the calcium in this drink. It is great for people who need more calcium.

Double Milk Banana Shake

1 banana, sliced
2/3 cup milk (skim or whole)
3 tablespoons skim milk powder
1/4 teaspoon flavoring (banana or vanilla)
2 teaspoons sugar

Slice banana; place in blender. Add other ingredients. Whip. Serves 1.

Strawberry Yogurt Shake

1 cup yogurt
1 cup strawberries
1/2 cup orange juice
1 tablespoon honey

Wash and hull strawberries. Place in blender or food processor. Add other ingredients. Whip.

Peanutty Punch

1 cup milk
2 tablespoons peanut butter
1 teaspoon honey
Dash nutmeg

Place all ingredients in blender; whip. One serving.

"Breakfast makes good memory."

Rabelais, *Gargantua*

Fast Breakfasts

Broiled Grapefruit
Whole Wheat Toast
Milk

Broiled Grapefruit

½ grapefruit per serving
Mint jelly (if desired)
Brown sugar

Wash grapefruit; slice in half. Cut out center, removing seeds. Sprinkle a small amount of brown sugar on top. Broil until sugar melts. Place a teaspoon of mint jelly in the center if desired. Serve warm.

"He that would eat a good dinner, let him eat a good breakfast."
Unknown

Apple-Peanut Butter Sandwich
Milk

Apple-Peanut Butter Sandwich

Apple **Peanut butter**

Wash apple. Remove seeds with apple corer. Cut off any blemish, but do not peel.

Slice crosswise to form circles.

For each sandwich: spread a slice with peanut butter; top with another apple slice.

"He that eats well does his work well."

Scottish Proverb, 1721

"Give us this day our daily bread."

Luke 11:13

Frozen Pancake or Waffle
Hot Cocoa

Pop the waffle into the toaster. Heat the cocoa—you are ready to eat.

Plan to keep this cocoa mix on hand. It is delicious for a bedtime snack as well as a breakfast food.

Cocoa Mix

3/4 cup cocoa
6 cups nonfat dry milk powder
3/4 cup sugar

Place all ingredients into a jar or canister. Shake or stir to blend. Store covered, away from heat. Use as desired.

To prepare one cup cocoa: Combine 1/3 cup cocoa mix and 3/4 cup water. Bring to boil. Serve warm.

"Only dull people are brilliant at breakfast."
Oscar Wilde, *An Ideal Husband*

4
Time-Saving Appliances

Three appliances are real time-savers in the kitchen. None of them is essential in order to cook delicious food. But for convenience, they offer benefits in the kitchen of busy people.

The food processor, freezer, and microwave oven are briefly discussed in this book with hints for use of each.

The microwave oven and a freezer enhance the value of each other.

The freezer keeps food (purchased or home prepared) fresh until it is needed.

The microwave thaws and heats frozen foods in minutes.

The combined appliances are time-saving winners.

"Lost yesterday, somewhere between sunrise and sunset, two golden hours, each set with sixty diamond minutes. No reward is offered, for they are gone forever."

Sigourney

"Well arranged time is the surest mark of a well arranged mind."

Pitman

Freeze with Ease

A freezer used to its fullest extent is a great time-saver.

You might ask, "How can a freezer help me fix food fast?" Obviously the freezer is not used for food preparation.

Learning to simplify food preparation and to use less time in grocery shopping are two secrets of time management for quick cooking.

A freezer used efficiently can save time and money plus be a great convenience.

Plan ahead and simplify your daily routine by using the freezer's capabilities.

1. Keep on hand enough food for one or two complete meals. That way, you know that no matter how rushed you are or who needs to be fed, there is something good to eat in the house which can be prepared fast.
2. Save time and money, and eat nutritious lunches at school and work by freezing foods ahead of time for daily brown-bagging.

   You can make five servings of dessert or salad in about the same time it takes to make one, but there is only one clean-up time.

   See the chapter "Brown Bagging" in this book for menu ideas which freeze well.
3. Keep a variety of breads on hand. Most bread will keep several months when frozen.

   English muffins, whole-wheat bread, biscuits, frozen patty shells, rolls, bagels, etc. are nice to have on hand. Ask yourself, "What types of breads do we like?"

4. Make a list of basic frozen foods you want to keep in the freezer: steaks, breads, fruits, vegetables, cakes, pies, etc. As you use one of your basic supplies, write it on a grocery list. That way you will always have a basic supply of foods you like in the freezer.

   When you have basic foods on hand, you have the freedom to expand a meal when family or friends drop in, as well as the convenience of daily use.
5. A freezer allows you to purchase foods in quantity. Meat can be bought on sale and stored for future use. This saves money and time (fewer trips to the store).
6. Many foods freeze well. Plan ahead, and freeze planned-over foods for future use.

   These foods could be: leftover meats which are sliced and frozen for later meals; uncooked casseroles (make one and freeze one) which can be cooked when needed; frozen pie or cake (purchased or homemade); spaghetti and meatballs (double the recipe), etc.

   It is time-saving to double a recipe and freeze half of it for future use. Two pies can be made in approximately the same time as one. The extra pie can be frozen and used on a day when there is no way you have time to cook a pie.
7. A purchased entrée plus a fruit, vegetable, and bread from the freezer make a super speedy, nutritious meal.

Hospitality in a Hurry

If you know you will have guests on a certain day, cook and freeze food several days in advance so that on the day of the party, you will be free to do last-minute details.

Special holiday or anniversary cakes keep well frozen.

Cookies and sweet rolls keep well.

Party sandwiches for receptions can be made weeks in advance.

Don't forget to freeze extra ice cubes in advance.

Rotate Frozen Foods

Keep your freezer as well stocked as possible. A variety of foods on hand ensures a good selection.

A nearly full freezer also uses less electricity than a nearly empty one.

Having said that, let me say that food should not be kept indefinitely in a freezer. Frozen foods have limited shelf time just as canned foods do. Plan to rotate foods on the shelves.

For best taste and quality, be sure frozen foods are stored in vapor-moisture-proof material and used within a reasonable time frame.

Suggested Storage Time for Frozen Foods

Precooked Foods

This includes foods which were commercially cooked and frozen as well as home-cooked foods.

Remember that purchased frozen foods have been in the store freezer too.

Fried chicken keeps four months.

Cooked chicken or turkey covered with broth keeps six months.

Cooked chicken or turkey not covered with broth keeps one month.

Never store turkey dressing in the bird. Remove the stuffing; package it; then freeze. It will not keep well frozen in a turkey.

Cooked lamb keeps two to three months.

Cooked fish keeps one month.

Cooked beef keeps two to three months.

Cooked fresh pork keeps two to three months.

Cooked cured ham keeps one to two months.

Meatballs in spaghetti sauce keep two to four months.

Beef, turkey, or chicken pies keep two to three months.

Stews and soups keep two to four months.
Casseroles keep three to six months.
Baked beans keep six months.
Sandwiches keep one month.
Pies keep four to six months.
Biscuits keep one month.
Cakes keep four to six months.
Breads keep six to eight months.
Ice cream keeps one to two months.

Fresh Frozen Foods

This includes foods which were commercially fresh frozen as well as home frozen.

Vegetables keep nine to twelve months.
Fruits keep nine to twelve months.
Fish keeps six to eight months.
Oysters and clams keep three to six months.
Shrimp keeps two months.
Fresh beef keeps six to twelve months.
Fresh ground beef keeps two to three months.
Fresh veal keeps six to nine months.
Fresh ground veal keeps two to three months.
Fresh pork keeps three to six months.
Fresh whole ham keeps two months.
Fresh ground pork keeps one to two months.
Steaks and chops keep three to four months.
Frankfurters keep one month.
Cheeses (Cheddar, Swiss, Parmesan) keep six months.
Fresh cream keeps one month.
Butter
  Salted keeps three months.
  Unsalted keeps six months.
Nutmeats keep one year.
Canapes keep one month.
Cookie dough keeps three months.

Unless the package is damaged, keep commercially frozen foods in their original packages.

Suggestions for How to Freeze Cooked Foods

All foods to be kept more than a day should be packaged in moisture-vapor-proof wrappings. These may be freezer plastic, foil, or paper.

Cakes

Cakes freeze well—both iced and uniced.

Freshly baked cakes should be cooled before freezing.

Cookies

Baked cookies should be baked, cooked, then wrapped.

Unbaked cookies can also be frozen:

1. Cut-out cookie dough is frozen by layering two pieces of waxed paper between cookies. (This prevents cookies from sticking together.)

Bake whenever fresh cookies are needed.

2. Drop cookies can be dropped on a baking sheet; the sheet is then placed in the freezer until cookies are firm.

Store up to three months in freezer wrap.

Pies

Baked and unbaked pies can be frozen. A pie which will be frozen, then baked, is wrapped with moisture-proof wrapping, then baked when needed.

Always freeze pies in a pie pan.

Breads

Biscuits—baked

Bake, cook, cool, wrap, and freeze.

If freezing cooked biscuits, I usually undercook them slightly, then complete the browning when they are heated.

Biscuits—unbaked

Prepare dough, roll out, cut out, then freeze.

Remove from the freezer when needed and place into a 450° oven.

Bread and rolls—baked

These will keep in a purchased package several days. If keeping them several months, store in freezer packaging.

Bread and rolls—unbaked

Yeast dough can be made, then rolls placed into baking pans as if they were to be baked immediately.

Allow rolls to rise; freeze; wrap. Bake as usual when needed. They keep well only one week.

Casseroles

Many casseroles freeze well. Freeze in a pan for later baking.

or

If you need the pan and do not wish to leave it in the freezer, freeze the casserole in a container (metal is best) until the contents are firm. Then heat the pan just enough to unstick the frozen casserole. Remove the pan; then package the frozen casserole. At this stage it will be like a block of ice, therefore easy to wrap.

When ready to bake the casserole, unwrap it, place it into the same pan, and bake.

Do not bake bread or cakes in dull, blackened pans. The baked products will burn on the bottom before they are done on top.

Bright aluminum pans are best for cakes, but if other containers are used, such as glass, lower the oven temperature 25 degrees.

Freeze with Ease Recipes

Nothing is simpler than planning ahead, so that on busy days you can enjoy meals requiring little preparation.

This book has numerous quick-cook recipes that freeze well. Scan through the pages, or see the Index for ideas.

Listed here are some suggestions. See the Index for page numbers.

Also listed are some recipes which freeze well, yet are not quick-cook foods.

Entrees

Broiled Chicken Breasts
Turkey Breast Steaks
Sauteed Chicken Livers
Anchovy-Cream Cheese
Pimento Cheese Spread
Ham and Date Rolls
Deviled Ham-Cream Cheese Sandwich
Roast pork, chicken, beef, veal
Baked Ham

Breads

Banana Muffins
Garlic Bread
Most purchased breads
More than Cornbread

Zucchini-Carrot Bread

1½ cups flour
¼ teaspoon baking powder
½ teaspoon soda
1 teaspoon cinnamon
1 teaspoon nutmeg
½ teaspoon salt
1 teaspoon vanilla
2 eggs
1 cup sugar
½ cup oil
½ cup pecans, chopped
½ cup grated carrots
½ cup grated zucchini

Preheat oven to 350°F.

Sift dry ingredients; set aside.

Beat eggs; add sugar; blend well. Add the oil, then carrots and zucchini.

Blend in dry ingredients, vanilla, and nuts. Pour into a greased 8 x 4 x 2 /12 inch loaf pan. Bake 60 minutes.

Hint: If you have a food processor, chop the nuts, set aside; then grate the carrots and zucchini; set them aside. Change to the metal blade and blend all the ingredients as instructed above. You will find the food processor a big time-saver.

Buttermilk Biscuits

This recipe calls for using the food processor to mix the biscuits. A processor saves time, but they can be made by hand in a short time also.

6 cups self-rising flour
1½ teaspoons soda
⅓ cup plus 1 tablespoon shortening
2¼ cups buttermilk

Sift flour and soda. Place into the bowl of a food processor with the blade; add shortening.

Pulse on and off 6 or 7 times until the consistency of meal.

Add milk *slowly*. You might not need all the milk. (The

amount of humidity in the air affects the amount of liquid needed.)

Pulse until blended, but do not overcombine. Quick breads such as biscuits become tough if overbeaten.

Empty dough onto a floured cloth; roll out. Cut into biscuits.

Place on an ungreased cookie sheet and bake 10 minutes in a 450° oven.

or

Place on a cookie sheet. Set into the freezer until firm. Then wrap unbaked biscuits for freezing.

Whenever you want one or more biscuits, reach into the freezer, get the number of unbaked biscuits needed, then place into a 450°F. oven to bake—Presto! Fresh-baked biscuits.

Apricot Bran Muffins

4 eggs
1 cup oil
1 (15 oz.) box wheat bran flakes cereal
1 quart buttermilk
1 cup chopped dried apricots

5 cups flour
1 teaspoon salt
5 teaspoons soda
1/2 teaspoon mace
3 cups sugar

Sift flour, salt, soda, and mace; set aside.

Beat eggs; add sugar, buttermilk, and oil. Blend in the cereal, then dry ingredients. Add apricots last.

Bake in greased muffin pans in a 400°F. oven 15 minutes.

Hint: This whole recipe can be baked at one time, freezing the surplus muffins.

or

The muffin mixture may be covered and stored in the refrigerator, ready to be used as needed. It keeps well for several days.

Cheese Muffins

1 cup sifted flour
1 cup cornmeal
1 teaspoon salt
2½ teaspoons baking powder
2 tablespoons sugar
⅔ cup grated Cheddar cheese
1 egg
1 cup milk
2 tablespoons bacon drippings

Preheat oven to 400°F.

Combine dry ingredients with cheese. Beat egg. Add all ingredients together; stir just enough to mix, but do not beat. Batter will be lumpy.

Pour into greased muffin pans. Bake 25 minutes. Makes 12 muffins.

Hint: Add a little chopped Jalapeno pepper to the batter if you like a hot Mexican-type bread.

DESSERTS

Peanut Butter Balls
Banana on a Stick
Honey Nut Spice Cake
Doughnuts
Cakes
Pies

Crispy Ice Cream Pie

1½ cups crisp rice cereal
1 cup miniature marshmallows
¼ cup milk
1 tablespoon butter
1 quart ice cream

Combine the marshmallows, milk, and butter; melt on low heat. When melted, fold in the rice cereal. Stir to coat the cereal.

Pour the cereal mixture into a greased 1½ quart flat container (such as a pie pan). Press on the sides and bottom with a spoon.

Slightly soften ice cream; then spoon on top of the crust. Freeze until firm. Serves 6 to 8.

Frozen Peanut Butter Dessert

This is an incredibly rich dessert, so plan to serve small portions.

It will keep for weeks in a freezer if wrapped.

3/4 cup crunchy peanut butter
1/2 cup honey
8 oz. cream cheese
2 cups frozen whipped topping
Vanilla ice cream
1 graham cracker pie crust

Combine the peanut butter, honey, and cream cheese; whip to blend. (I use a food processor with the dough blade.)

Add the whipped topping. Pour mixture into a graham cracker pie crust. Freeze until firm.

Soften ice cream slightly; spoon on top of the frozen peanut butter mixture. Place back in the freezer.

To serve: Slice small pie wedge portions; allow to slightly soften before eating.

Graham Cracker Crust

1 1/2 cups graham cracker crumbs
1/4 cup margarine or butter
1 tablespoon sugar

Combine ingredients. Press into the bottom of a 9-inch pie pan. Bake in a 350° oven 6-8 minutes. Remove from oven; let cool.

Ice Cream Pie

1 graham cracker crust (see previous recipe or purchase)
Butternut sauce, if desired (see Index)
Vanilla ice cream

Slightly soften ice cream. Fill pie crust with cream; freeze firm. Top with butternut sauce.

Cheesecake

1 can (14 oz.) sweetened condensed milk
¼ cup sour cream
2 (8 oz.) packages cream cheese
3 eggs
1 teaspoon lemon extract
¼ cup lemon juice

Place sweetened condensed milk, sour cream, and cream cheese into the bowl of a food processor or mixer. Whip to combine. Add the eggs and beat; then add lemon juice and extract.

Pour into a springform pan which is lined with graham cracker crust (see Index).

Bake approximately 55 minutes—until the center springs back when touched. Cool; chill in the refrigerator or freeze for future use.

"Beauty of style and harmony and grace . . . depend on simplicity."

Plato

Points on Processors

Although a food processor is not a necessity for people who cook in a hurry, it is a desirable appliance. It does not cook food, but it can save an enormous amount of time with food preparation.

The time needed for grating, slicing, blending, etc., can be cut to seconds.

Many quick-cook recipes call for cutting food into small pieces because food cut into segments cooks faster than the same food left whole.

It is conservation of time and energy that makes a food processor so valuable. You can slice, dice, chop, shred, combine, and blend with the touch of a finger.

A food processor does not enhance food flavor. Food cut by hand or machine will taste the same.

A blender can be used to do many of the same things as a food processor, but it has to be watched more closely. A blender tends to cut food too fine for most recipes. It also holds smaller quantities than a processor.

The cook might find a food processor is not time-efficient for some recipes. If the only thing a processor is used for in a meal is to slice an onion or chop one stalk of celery, a knife should be used. It requires less time to wash. But if a processor can be used in preparation of several foods, or has multiple uses in one recipe, it is much more efficient than hand methods.

The fastest way to prepare food is to learn to use a processor for several steps in meal preparation.

To maximize quick food preparation and decrease dish washing: Slice or chop large dry ingredients first (such as nuts and cheese); set them aside. Then mix dry ingredients (such as flour, baking powder, soda, spices, etc.); set them aside. Combine eggs, butter, sugar, etc. in the bowl next; then add liquid and dry ingredients.

All of this can be done in seconds if you get in the habit of using the appliance in a time-efficient manner.

Hints for Using the Food Processor

1. Meats can be sliced or julienned using disks or diced using the metal blade.

   Fresh meat slices better if slightly frozen. It is stiffer, therefore easier to cut.

   Cooked meats slice better when cool.
2. Pulse on and off to get even dicing of food. It will also prevent overprocessing. Use the metal blade to dice meat, fruit, vegetables, and nuts.
3. Use the processor to prepare frequently used ingredients; then store them in the refrigerator for future use. For instance, chopped onions, parsley, shallots, and peppers can be tightly covered and kept up to a week in the refrigerator.

   Garlic, shallots, and onions keep well when covered with salad oil, then stored in a covered jar. These vegetables not only keep well, but the oil is great used in salad dressing or for seasoned cooking oil.
4. To shred a whole salad such as slaw at one time, use a shredding disk, and place all the vegetables in the feeder tube at the same time.

   If food will not fit into the top of the feed tube, cut it into smaller pieces, or fill the tube from the bottom. It is slightly larger from the bottom.

   You can often fit a whole salad in from the bottom.
5. When using a slicing disk:

   Press firmly on the pusher if you want thick slices.

   Use little pressure if you want thin slices.

Memo on the Microwave

The fastest expanding market in the appliance industry is the microwave oven. It fits the needs and life-style of small families who need to cook in a hurry.

The addition of a microwave to the kitchen expands quick-cook possibilities. And this book includes a number of quick-cook recipes for microwave meals in minutes.

It is a real time saver in the kitchen, but it is not a "souped-up" version of the kitchen range.

Persons owning a microwave will be better satisfied if they realize the oven offers more options, but has not replaced all old methods.

This book has a multitude of innovative ways to cook food fast using a standard range. Some foods taste better cooked in the microwave; others have better color, texture, and taste with traditional methods.

When preparing a whole meal (other than frozen food or reheating leftovers), I usually find it saves time to combine the microwave and conventional range. That way you can cook several things at one time and cook large quantities too—if needed.

The microwave oven, like the food processor, has to be seen to be believed, and must be used to understand how it cuts cooking time.

Time-Saving Tips

Vegetables cooked in a microwave tend to retain color and texture better than most vegetables cooked with traditional methods.

Vegetables are usually cooked covered with little water

added. Liquid does not evaporate as much in a microwave as in coventional cooking. Two to four tablespoons of water is usually enough to cook fresh vegetables.

Salt sometimes toughens vegetables. For best texture, salt after removing from oven.

All foods (vegetables, fruits, meats) should be cut into uniform size pieces for even cooking. If food is cut into a mixture of large and small pieces, the small pieces will be done before the large ones cook.

Most frozen vegetables and fruits should be thawed before cooking. To thaw: Place food in the oven icy side up. Set microwave on low or defrost. Microwaves defrost the icy outside of the food first; then heat travels to the inside. As the food defrosts, break it up with a fork—it will defrost more evenly and faster.

Whole vegetables or fruits which have skins should be pricked several times before cooking. Otherwise a buildup of steam could cause them to explode.

Never boil an egg in a microwave oven. It, too, will explode and make a mess. Even an egg yolk will explode, so pierce the membrane which covers the yolk before cooking. Scrambled eggs cook beautifully.

Most pastry and breads which are made from scratch look and taste better if cooked in a conventional oven. These foods need to be browned, and a microwave cannot do that.

The microwave is ideal for thawing a frozen pie which was precooked before freezing.

Another way to cook a pie with a pastry crust is to cook it a short time in the microwave, then brown it in an oven as it completes cooking. Total baking time will be less than using a conventional oven alone.

Of course, pies can be made with crusts other than pastry. Graham cracker, gingersnap, and chocolate wafer crumb crusts are delicious and can be made in one or two minutes in a microwave.

Cakes and cookies baked in a microwave cannot brown on the outside and be soft inside as they are in a traditional oven. They will be either soft all the way through or crisp all the way through.

Since baked goods do not brown well, dessert recipes for use in the microwave oven have dark ingredients such as molasses, brown sugar, and spices to add color. There are a lot of good baked dessert recipes for use in the microwave which use these ingredients.

When one is baking a cake, the baking pan is usually greased but not floured. (Microwaving leaves a layer of flour on the cake bottom.)

Fruit desserts cook well in the microwave. Even dried fruits such as raisins, apricots, and peaches plump up beautifully.

To plump up a small bowl of raisins: Add water to nearly cover raisins in a small bowl; loosely cover bowl; microwave one minute.

Meringue shells cannot be baked in the oven. They need a long, slow baking. Use the traditional oven for meringue toppings and shells.

Purchased sauces (for ice cream or cake) can be heated in seconds for a dessert topping. Even jellies and jams can be warmed for quick, sweet toppings.

Foods with a high amount of sugar and fat get very hot and cook quickly. Foods low in fat and sugar tend to have longer cooking times.

Cooking time needed can vary for the same recipe. A microwave oven with low wattage takes longer to cook than one with 600-700 watts. Food temperature when placed in the oven also affects length of cooking time. Food which is at room temperature cooks quicker than the same food straight out of the refrigerator. For example, a casserole which has been prepared for cooking, then stored in the refrigerator until cooking time, will take longer to bake than the same casserole takes if all ingredients are at room temperature. The quantity of food cooked also affects time needed. Small quantities cook much faster than large.

Since the quantity of food cooked, food temperature, and

type of microwave oven used affect cooking time, a good rule of thumb is: Remove food from the oven before it is completely done. Foods continue to cook for a short time after removal from the oven.

If food cooking in a microwave starts to boil over, open the door and it will stop.

Should food catch on fire, cut the oven off, but leave the door closed until the fire goes out.

Rice and pasta take a long time to cook in a microwave and require stirring several times. A traditional cooking method probably takes no more time and requires less stirring.

Cooked rice and pasta can be warmed up for eating in seconds or used in a casserole. When cooking these cereals, prepare enough so the leftovers can be heated in the microwave.

Meat cooked in a microwave should be tender cuts or should be marinated before cooking. The microwave cooks too fast to tenderize meat.

Small roasts cook better than large ones. If a roast is over one inch thick, turn it over during cooking to ensure even roasting.

Meat, like fruit and vegetables, cooks faster in thin spots than thick. Try to have roasts, chops, and so on uniform in thickness.

If you must cook meat of uneven size, such as chicken legs, place the thick sides of drumsticks toward the outside of the pan. Food near the outside edge cooks faster than food near the pan's center.

Meat continues to cook after it is removed from the oven. Therefore, remove it from oven before completely done. Let a roast sit five to ten minutes before eating.

Meat loaf cooks faster in a ring mold than in a loaf pan.

When cooking poultry, start cooking with the skin side down. Turn it over halfway through the cooking period. A whole chicken should first be placed breast down, then turned.

Microwave recipes usually require stirring or repositioning of food while it cooks because food near the edge of a pan cooks faster than food in the center. Food is also repositioned to ensure even microwave penetration.

Round pans are better for cooking than square because food cooks faster in corners.

Containers with straight sides cook more evenly than pans with sloping edges.

Never use glass containers with small mouths (such as vinegar or syrup jar) in the microwave. Food could heat and expand so quickly that the top would break.

Never use metal containers. At best they cause uneven cooking; but worse is the danger of oven damage.

Oven thermometers for standard ranges must not be used. Mercury is in most thermometers, and it will damage a microwave oven.

5
Cheese Is a Breeze

Cheese is a fabulous fast food. It is used frequently in this book because it is a nutritious, delicious food which is simple to serve.

A dessert of Camembert, fruit, and coffee speaks of simple elegance and relaxed conversation after a long day at the office.

Cheese can be used as an accompaniment, appetizer, main course, or dessert. Most of the time it requires little preparation. Even when it is "cooked" in a main-course dish, the preparation is usually just slicing or grating.

Groceries and specialty food shops have an enormous variety of cheeses on display.

Since cheese is eaten around the world, a trip to the cheese counter can be an adventure. There is no need to be intimidated by exotic foreign names. The cheese chart in this chapter lists names, pronunciations, tastes, and uses of most of the cheeses you would encounter. Until you become familiar with new names, refer to it often.

Cheese is a concentrated food, so a little bit goes a long way. Usually it is an economical meat substitute since one or two ounces is adequate for a serving.

Nutritious

Twenty to thirty percent of the total weight of natural cheese is protein. It is a complete protein, which means it has all the amino acids needed to build body cells.

Cheese is also rich in bone-building calcium, phosphorus, and vitamin D, plus vitamin A and riboflavin (B_2).

Cheeses have fat in them. Some have less fat than others—for example, lowfat Cottage, Pot, and Farmers. If you wish to lower your fat and caloric intake, choose one of the low-fat cheeses. When cheese is used as a meat substitute, you might wish to compare how much fat you would eat in a serving of meat vs. a serving of cheese—often about the same.

Natural cheese is made from milk. It can come from various animals, but usually it is from a cow or goat.

Taste and texture in cheeses vary a great deal because of the type milk used and how long the cheeses are aged. A mild Cheddar is aged two to three months; a medium ages three to six months; and a full-bodied sharp is over six months old.

Cheese is made by removing liquid whey from sour milk. A cheese can be made from whole milk, whole milk with cream added, a combination of milk and whey, etc.

Obviously cheese made from milk and cream (cream cheese) has more calories than lowfat cheese (lowfat cottage).

Delicious

Most cheeses improve in flavor if left to set at room temperature for 15-60 minutes before eating. Therefore, if you plan to serve one for a snack, appetizer, or dessert, set it out when you start preparing other food.

To prevent drying out, keep the cheese covered as it comes to room temperature. Plastic wrap, aluminum foil, and a cheese dish all make good covers.

Cheeses which improve in taste at room temperature are:

Cheddar
Colby
Brick
Blue
Edam
Gorgonzola
Gouda
Monterey (Jack)
Muenster
Port du Salut
Provolone
Swiss

Soft cheeses should be left at room temperature a short time before eating. They are:

Brie	Cream
Bel Paese	Neufchatel
Camembert	Ricotta
Cottage	

Fix It Fast

Process cheese melts easily. Just chop it and add to food being cooked such as a sauce or casserole.

Shred or grate Cheddar; keep it tightly covered in the refrigerator. It comes in handy for a topping on casseroles, salads, and desserts. And it will always be there for a quick pimento cheese sandwich.

A food processor is a great time-saver for grating or slicing cheese. A blender will do; it just takes longer.

Cheese which is cold is easier to grate.

Very hard cheese such as Romano and Parmesan can be grated by hand, blender, or fed through small hold into the food processor, using the metal blade for grating.

The fastest method for adding cheese to food being cooked is to simply dice or chop it. Use a knife, blender, or processor to chop.

Always cook cheese at a low temperature since high heat toughens it.

To slice cheese for appetizers or dessert, set out a small knife or cheese cutter. Let everybody cut their own.

Cheese Chart

Starting on page 150 is a descriptive cheese chart. It lists types, tastes, textures, and uses of most cheeses plus pronunciation of their names.

"Feed me with food convenient for me."

Proverbs 30:8

TYPE	PRONUNCIATION	TASTE TEXTURE	USES
Bel Paese	bell pah ch zeh	A type of Brie. Italian origin. It is a creamy, mild-flavored cheese with a waxy body.	Appetizer, dessert, snacks. Eat with fruit or crackers.
Blue	bloo	Tangy taste. White cheese with blue-green veins. It is similar to Roquefort. Blue is made from cow's milk, Roquefort from the milk of sheep. Blue cheese originated in U.S.	Appetizer, dessert, salad, salad dressing, snacks. Serve with fruit or crackers for appetizer or dessert.
Brick	brik	Mild to sharp flavor. Brick shaped with brownish exterior and small interior holes.	Appetizer, dessert, sandwich, snacks. Good with fruit.
Brie	bree	Mild to pungent taste. It has an edible tan crust and soft interior. Origin was France. Made in U.S. now. Bel Paese is a type of brie.	Appetizer, dessert, snack. Good with fruit or crackers.
Caciocavallo	ca cheo ca-val lo	A hard cheese with an agreeably pungent, salty flavor.	Appetizer, cooking, dessert, snacks. Grate if aged.
Camembert	kam em bear	Soft cheese with smooth texture and slightly tangy flavor. The gray-white crust is edible. Serve at room temperature for full flavor. Originated in France. If the exterior has turned brown and it has an ammonia flavor, it is past its prime.	Appetizer, dessert, snack. Good with fruit or crackers.

TYPE	PRONUNCIATION	TASTE TEXTURE	USES
Cheddar	ched ar	It can be mild, medium, or sharp—depending on how long it is aged. A good sharp cheese is aged for 6 months or more. The texture is firm to crumbly, and the color is usually creamy yellow. It comes in several shapes and styles. Longhorn, New York State, Monterey Jack, and Wisconsin are all Cheddar cheese. American cheese is made from either Cheddar or Colby cheese.	Appetizer, cooking, dessert, sandwich, snacks.
Colby	cole be	Much like Cheddar. It has a mild flavor, soft body, and fairly open texture.	Cooking, sandwich, snacks.
Cottage	kot ij	Soft, moist, uncured cheese with slightly acid flavor. It can have large or small curds and can be regular or lowfat cottage cheese.	Cooking, salad, salad dressing, snack.
Cream	krem	A soft, uncured cheese with a slightly acid flavor with butter-like texture. Its bland flavor and smooth texture combine well with many foods.	Appetizer, dessert, sandwich, snacks, salad.
Edam	e dam	A mild, mellow cheese. It is round in form with a red coat—beautiful on a cheese tray.	Appetizer, dessert, salad, sandwich, snacks. Slice in wedges, or scoop cheese out of the shell.
Fontinci	fon te na	A yellow, salty, strong-flavored cheese.	Appetizer, dessert. Serve with crackers and fruit or grate when mature and hard.

TYPE	PRONUNCIATION	TASTE TEXTURE	USES
Formazgini di Lecco	fohr makd ah-jene de la co	An Italian cheese much like cream cheese.	Dessert. Mix cream and sugar with it for a dessert spread.
Gjetost	yet ost	Scandinavian cheese (Norway) with a butter-like consistency and sweet flavor.	Appetizer, dessert, snack. Try sliced thin on dark bread.
Gorgonzola	gor gon zo la	An Italian cheese made from cow's milk. It has a strong, tangy flavor and crumbly texture. It is white with blue veins. It is similar to Blue cheese.	Appetizer, dessert, salad, snack. Serve on fruit or crackers.
Gouda	goo da	It is similar to Edam, but is softer and milder. It has a red wax coating.	Appetizer, dessert, salad, sandwich, snack. Cut into wedges or scoop out. Great with fruit.
Gruyere	grew yare	A cheese which originated in Switzerland and is similar to Swiss cheese. It is pale yellow with small holes and has a sharp flavor.	Appetizer, dessert, salad, snack.
Liederkranz	le dar krants	An American cheese which is soft creamy white with a pungent flavor.	Appetizer, dessert. Set foil-wrapped rectangle on tray with fruit or crackers.
Limburger	lim bur gar	A creamy white cheese with a strong odor and flavor. Keep in an airtight container in the refrigerator.	Appetizer, sandwich, snacks. Serve with dark bread or pretzels.
Monterey Jack	mon ta ra	A type of Cheddar. It is hard when aged, but usually it is slightly soft.	Appetizer, cooking, dessert, sandwich.

TYPE	PRONUNCIATION	TASTE TEXTURE	USES
Mozzarella	mottza rel la	Creamy white, mild, plastic textured cheese. When you think of pizzas, Mozzarella is the cheese to choose.	Cooking, sandwiches.
Muenster	mun stir	A cheese which is pungent, but mild. It is creamy-white with a tan coat. It originated in Germany, now made in U.S.	Appetizer, dessert, snack. Serve with fruit or crackers.
Mysost	mews ost	A sweet cheese of Scandinavian origin. It is light brown and butter-like.	Appetizer, dessert, snack.
Neufchatel	new sha tel	A creamy, uncured, mild cheese much like Cream Cheese. It has less butter fat and more moisture than Cream Cheese—a whey cheese.	Dessert, cooking, salad, sandwich, snack.
Parmesan	par mi zan	A sharp-flavored, hard cheese.	Grate for cooking.
Port du Salut	pore du sa loo	A creamy yellow cheese with a mild to robust flavor. It has a fairly strong odor.	Appetizer, dessert, snack. Serve with fruit or crackers.
Provolone	pro vo lo na	A hard cheese with an agreeably pungent flavor which varies from mild to sharp.	Appetizer, cooking, dessert, sandwich, snack. Serve with fruit.
Ricotta	ri cot ah	A bland, white cheese. It can be moist with loose curds or hard enough to grate. Lowfat Ricotta can be purchased and is a good low-calorie cheese.	Desserts, cooking, salad.

TYPE	PRONUNCIATION	TASTE TEXTURE	USES
Romano	ro ma no	A very sharp, hard cheese with a firm texture. It has a yellowish white interior and black or brown coating.	Appetizer, snack. Up to 8 months of age, use like Cheddar. If aged 8 months or more, grate and use as Parmesan.
Roquefort	rok fart	This cheese is made in France from sheep's milk. It is white with blue-green veins and has a piquant flavor which leaves a pleasant bouquet in the mouth.	Appetizer, dessert, served with fruit or crackers or Use crumbled in salad and salad dressing.
Sapsago	sap sa go	Herbs are used when making this cheese; they give it a green color. It is hard textured with a mild to sharp flavor. Origin: Switzerland.	Grate for cooking.
Stilton	stil ton	A white cheese with green-blue veins. The flavor is much like Roquefort, except milder. It is made from cow's milk and Roquefort is made from sheep's milk. An excellent dessert choice.	Appetizer, dessert. Serve with fruit or crackers.
Swiss	swis	A firm cheese with an elastic body. The flavor is mild, nutlike. It has large holes formed by normal, natural gas explosions during the cheese making process.	Slice fairly thick for flavor. Use brown bread and serve as appetizer, sandwich, or snack.

Other Cheese Choices—Process Cheeses

Pasteurized Process Cheese is made from natural cheese which has been heated to its melting point, pasteurized, and mixed with an emulsifier.

Nearly half the cheese eaten in the United States is pasteurized process. The most popular variety is pasteurized process American cheese. It is made from natural Cheddar or Cheddar and Colby combined.

Once a cheese is pasteurized, it stops "aging." It stays the same flavor—usually fairly bland.

Some process cheeses have vegetable fat substituted for part of the animal fat.

Pasteurized Process Cheese Food is the same as process cheese except thinner. It has more milk and whey added to thin it. These also make it low in calories.

Cheese foods often are flavored with fruit, smoke, or vegetables.

Pasteurized Process Cheese Spread is manufactured the same way as pasteurized process cheese food except that enough milk and whey are added to make it a spread at room temperature.

Flavor is often added—smoke, fruit, etc.

Cold Pack or Club Cheeses have more of the original cheese taste than pasteurized cheeses. They are not heated, and no emulsifiers are added.

Club cheeses are made by grinding and blending natural cheese (often with vegetable or smoke flavor added) to make a spread.

Use them for appetizers, desserts, and sandwiches.

Cold Pack Cheese Foods are manufactured like Cold Pack Cheese except they have more milk and whey added; therefore, they are milder and thinner.

Sometimes corn syrup, meat, fruit, or vegetables are added to enhance the flavor.

INDEX